15 Days of Prayer
With The Curé of Ars

Also in the *15 Days of Prayer* collection:

15 DAYS OF PRAYER

WITH

The Curé of Ars

PIERRE BLANC

Translated by Victoria Hébert and Denis Sabourin

Liguori

LIGUORI, MISSOURI

Published by Liguori Publications
Liguori, Missouri
www.liguori.org
www.catholicbooksonline.com

This book is a translation of *Prier 15 Jours Avec Le Curé d'Ars*, published by Nouvelle Cité, 1995, Montrouge, France.

Library of Congress Cataloging-in-Publication Data

Blanc, Pierre.
    [Prier 15 jours avec le Curé d'Ars. English]
    15 days of prayer with the Curé of Ars / Pierre Blanc ; [translated by] Victoria Hébert and Denis Sabourin. — 1st English ed.
        p. cm.
    Includes bibliographical references.
    ISBN 0-7648-0713-7 (pbk.)
    1. Vianney, Jean Baptiste Marie, Saint, 1786–1859—Meditations. 2. Spiritual life—Catholic Church. I. Title: Fifteen days of prayer with the Curé of Ars.

BX4700.V5 B5713 2001
269'.6—dc21   2001029042

Printed in the United States of America
05 04 03 02 01 5 4 3 2 1
First English Edition 2001

Table of Contents

How to Use This Book

AN OLD CHINESE PROVERB, or at least what I am able to recall of what is supposed to be an old Chinese proverb, goes something like this: "Even a journey of a thousand miles begins with a single step." When you think about it, the truth of the proverb is obvious. It is impossible to begin any project, let alone a journey, without taking the first step. I think it might also be true, although I cannot recall if another Chinese proverb says it, "that the first step is often the hardest." Or, as someone else once observed, "the distance between a thought and the corresponding action needed to implement the idea takes the most energy." I don't know who shared that perception with me but I am certain it was not an old Chinese master!

With this ancient proverbial wisdom, and the not-so-ancient wisdom of an unknown contemporary sage still fresh, we move from proverbs to presumptions. How do these relate to the task before us?

I am presuming that if you are reading this introduction it is because you are contemplating a journey. My presumption is that you are preparing for a spiritual journey and that you have taken at least some of the first steps necessary to prepare for this journey. I also presume, and please excuse me if I am making too many presumptions, that in your preparation for the spiritual journey you have determined that you need a guide.

From deep within the recesses of your deepest self, there was something that called you to consider Saint John Vianney as a potential companion. If my presumptions are correct, may I congratulate you on this decision? I think you have made a wise choice, a choice that can be confirmed by yet another source of wisdom, the wisdom that comes from practical experience.

Even an informal poll of experienced travelers will reveal a common opinion; it is very difficult to travel alone. Some might observe that it is even foolish. Still others may be even stronger in their opinion and go so far as to insist that it is necessary to have a guide, especially when you are traveling into uncharted waters and into territory that you have not yet experienced. I am of the personal opinion that a traveling companion is welcome under all circumstances. The thought of traveling alone, to some exciting destination without someone to share the journey with does not capture my imagination or channel my enthusiasm. However, with that being noted, what is simply a matter of preference on the normal journey becomes a matter of necessity when a person embarks on a spiritual journey.

The spiritual journey, which can be the most challenging of all journeys, is experienced best with a guide, a companion, or at the very least, a friend in whom you have placed your trust. This observation is not a preference or an opinion but rather an established spiritual necessity. All of the great saints with whom I am familiar had a spiritual director or a confessor who journeyed with them. Admittedly, at times the saint might well have traveled far beyond the experience of their guide and companion but more often than not they would return to their director and reflect on their experience. Understood in this sense, the director and companion provided a valuable contribution and necessary resource.

When I was learning how to pray (a necessity for anyone who desires to be a full-time and public "religious person"), the community of men that I belong to gave me a great gift. Between my second and third year in college, I was given a one-year sabbatical, with all expenses paid and all of my personal needs met. This period of time was called novitiate. I was officially designated as a novice, a beginner in the spiritual journey, and I was assigned a "master," a person who was willing to lead me. In addition to the master, I was provided with every imaginable book and any other resource that I could possibly need. Even with all that I was provided, I did not learn how to pray because of the books and the unlimited resources, rather it was the master, the companion who was the key to the experience.

One day, after about three months of reading, of quiet and solitude, and of practicing all of the methods and descriptions of prayer that were available to me, the master called. "Put away the books, forget the method, and just listen." We went into a room, became quiet, and tried to recall the presence of God, and then, the master simply prayed out loud and permitted me to listen to his prayer. As he prayed, he revealed his hopes, his dreams, his struggles, his successes, and most of all, his relationship with God. I discovered as I listened that his prayer was deeply intimate but most of all it was self-revealing. As I learned about him, I was led through his life experience to the place where God dwells. At that moment I was able to understand a little bit about what I was supposed to do if I really wanted to pray.

The dynamic of what happened when the master called, invited me to listen, and then revealed his innermost self to me as he communicated with God in prayer, was important. It wasn't so much that the master was trying to reveal to me what needed to be said; he was not inviting me to pray with the same words that he used, but rather that he was trying to bring me to that place within myself where prayer becomes possible. That place, a place of intimacy and of self-awareness, was a necessary stop on the journey and it was a place that I needed to be led to. I could not have easily discovered it on my own.

The purpose of the volume that you hold in your hand is to lead you, over a period of fifteen days or, maybe more realistically, fifteen prayer periods, to a place where prayer is possible. If you already have a regular experience and practice of prayer, perhaps this volume can help lead you to a deeper place, a more intimate relationship with the Lord.

It is important to note that the purpose of this book is not to lead you to a better relationship with Saint John Vianney, your spiritual companion. Although your companion will invite you to share some of their deepest and most intimate thoughts, your companion is doing so only to bring you to that place where God dwells. After all, the true measurement of a companion for the journey is that they bring you to the place where you need to be, and then they step back, out of the picture. A guide who brings you to the desired destination and then sticks around is a very unwelcome guest!

Many times I have found myself attracted to a particular idea or method for accomplishing a task, only to discover that what seemed to be inviting and helpful possessed too many details. All of my energy went to the mastery of the details and I soon lost my enthusiasm. In each instance, the book that seemed so promising ended up on my bookshelf, gathering dust. I can assure you, it is not our intention that this book end up in your bookcase, filled with promise, but unable to deliver.

There are three simple rules that need to be followed in order to use this book with a measure of satisfaction.

Place: It is important that you choose a place for reading that provides the necessary atmosphere for reflection and that does not allow for too many distractions. Whatever place you choose needs to be comfortable, have the necessary lighting, and, finally, have a sense of "welcoming" about it. You need to be able to look forward to the experience of the journey. Don't travel steerage if you know you will be more comfortable in first class and if the choice is realistic for you. On the other hand, if first class is a distraction and you feel more comfortable and more yourself in steerage, then it is in steerage that you belong.

My favorite place is an overstuffed and comfortable chair in my bedroom. There is a light over my shoulder, and the chair reclines if I feel a need to recline. Once in a while, I get lucky and the sun comes through my window and bathes the entire room in light. I have other options and other places that are available to me but this is the place that I prefer.

Time: Choose a time during the day when you are most alert and when you are most receptive to reflection, meditation, and prayer. The time that you choose is an essential component. If you are a morning person, for example, you should choose a time that is in the morning. If you are more alert in the afternoon, choose an afternoon time slot; and if evening is your preference, then by all means choose the evening. Try to avoid "peak" periods in your daily routine when you know that you might be disturbed. The time that you choose needs to be your time and needs to work for you.

It is also important that you choose how much time you

will spend with your companion each day. For some it will be possible to set aside enough time in order to read and reflect on all the material that is offered for a given day. For others, it might not be possible to devote one time to the suggested material for the day, so the prayer period may need to be extended for two, three, or even more sessions. It is not important how long it takes you; it is only important that it works for you and that you remain committed to that which is possible.

For myself I have found that fifteen minutes in the early morning, while I am still in my robe and pajamas and before my morning coffee, and even before I prepare myself for the day, is the best time. No one expects to see me or to interact with me because I have not yet "announced" the fact that I am awake or even on the move. However, once someone hears me in the bathroom, then my window of opportunity is gone. It is therefore important to me that I use the time that I have identified when it is available to me.

Freedom: It may seem strange to suggest that freedom is the third necessary ingredient, but I have discovered that it is most important. By freedom I understand a certain "stance toward life," a "permission to be myself and to be gentle and understanding of who I am." I am constantly amazed at how the human person so easily sets himself or herself up for disappointment and perceived failure. We so easily make judgments about ourselves and our actions and our choices, and very often those judgments are negative, and not at all helpful.

For instance, what does it really matter if I have chosen a place and a time, and I have missed both the place and the time for three days in a row? What does it matter if I have chosen, in that twilight time before I am completely awake and still a little sleepy, to roll over and to sleep for fifteen minutes more? Does it mean that I am not serious about the journey, that I really don't want to pray, that I am just fooling myself when I say that my prayer time is important to me? Perhaps, but I prefer to believe that it simply means that I am tired and I just wanted a little more sleep. It doesn't mean anything more than that. However, if I make it mean more than that, then I can become discouraged, frustrated, and put myself into a state where I might more easily give up. "What's the use? I might as well forget all about it."

The same sense of freedom applies to the reading and the praying of this text. If I do not find the introduction to each day helpful, I don't need to read it. If I find the questions for reflection at the end of the appointed day repetitive, then I should choose to close the book and go my own way. Even if I discover that the reflection offered for the day is not the one that I prefer and that the one for the next day seems more inviting, then by all means, go on to the one for the next day.

That's it! If you apply these simple rules to your journey you should receive the maximum benefit and you will soon find yourself at your destination. But be prepared to be surprised. If you have never been on a spiritual journey you should know that the "travel brochures" and the other descriptions that you might have heard are nothing compared to the real thing. There is so much more than you can imagine.

A final prayer of blessing suggests itself:

> Lord, catch me off guard today.
> Surprise me with some moment of beauty
>   or pain
> So that at least for the moment
> I may be startled into seeing that you are
>   here in all your splendor,
> Always and everywhere,
> Barely hidden,
> Beneath,
> Beyond,
> Within this life I breathe.
>
> —*Frederick Buechner*

REV. THOMAS M. SANTA, CSsR
LIGUORI, MISSOURI
FEAST OF THE PRESENTATION, 1999

Introduction

I have nothing else to prove to you except the indispensable obligation we have to become saints (John Vianney).

THE SPIRITUAL ITINERARY that is proposed for the these fifteen days of personal retreat is a walk towards holiness with the secret desire that, as the days go by, each of us discovers with what love, with what immense love we have been loved by God; a love that is different and unique for each of us.

It is to discover that only one word is necessary so that the Lord amplifies his presence in us (without so much as suppressing our personality): *yes*. It is a yes that is complete and lived on a daily basis, just like the Blessed Virgin knew how to do and still helps us to do today through faith. In as much as we let God love us, and want to love him with all our heart, we rediscover that we cannot live just anything in any which way.

We are all called to holiness, and we must desire this holiness because it is the practical application of God's love for us. It is a complete union with God, our serious acceptance of our vocation and mission as baptized believers.

OUR ITINERARY

During the two first days we will align our lives with God by discovering what God's work is and what it means to love for him.

For the next two days, we will see that prayer is a living relationship with God, and that faithfulness to the Lord leads us to pass by the cross in Jesus' footsteps.

As our union with God is made stronger and stronger, we then see just how the Eucharist and reconciliation are extraordinary riches for our faith.

At the heart of our covenant of love with God, we will spend a day with Mary, the one who, filled with the Holy Spirit, fully said "yes" to the Father, in order to give the world Christ the Savior.

Then, for five days, we will deepen our way to live the Gospel: share our faith, welcome others, understand the place of the laity in the Church and live in a better way in the Church, and proclaim the Gospel; many roads on which the Curé of Ars will be our guide to help us grow in the love of God and our brothers and sisters.

Knowing that we live our relationship with God and others by means of who we are, we will meditate with John Vianney about life and the mission of Christian families and priests. These are two important days to follow the Curé of Ars, all the way to death and the definitive meeting with God.

In fact, the last day of prayer we will have together has the title "Death and Holiness." To meditate on death is not currently popular, but how necessary it is in order to fully live our Christian faith, whose foundation is the Resurrection of Jesus, the same one who "suffered under Pontius Pilate, was crucified, died…," as we say in the Apostles' Creed. Death leads to a life with God, a life with a full relationship for which we are already preparing on earth through our union with God and our human brothers and sisters.

This path of life is called *holiness*, and it is possible for each one of us through our welcome to the Holy Spirit. The Holy Spirit leads us, in as much as we want to live our baptism, to say a total yes to God, the Trinity of love, so that he will realize, in and through us, his will, his work: a progression of faith that we will live for our greater happiness and that of our brothers and sisters.

Those who love God are people who shake things up, for they put the way we live our life into question. They shake things up because "wherever the saints go, God goes with them..." (John Vianney). Let us then become saints!

Note: All of the citations in this book made by the Curé of Ars are taken from Father Bernard Nolet's book entitled *John Vianney, Curé of Ars, His Thoughts, His Heart (Jean-Marie Vianney, Curé d'Ars, sa pensée, son coeur)* (Mappus, 1960), as well as Father Nolet's collection entitled, *The Nicest Texts of the Curé of Ars' Catechisms (Les plus beaux texts des catéchismes du saint curé d'Ars)* (Publications Lyon-Trévoux, 1976).

A Brief Chronology of the Life of Saint John Vianney, the Curé of Ars

IT IS WITH SAINT JOHN VIANNEY, perhaps more well known under the title the Curé of Ars, that we will be spending the next fifteen days in prayer. But before beginning our spiritual journey, let us take some time to discover who this man was whose spiritual life radiated beyond the borders of his little village of Ars, spreading itself out to touch the entire world, eventually leading this "simple, common" parish priest to sainthood.

1786–1802:

> John Vianney was born on May 8, 1786, in Dardilly (near Lyons), in the province of Rhone, France. He was the fourth of six children, born to a farming family. His was a good Catholic family at a time when those who practiced had to do so in a clandestine manner; priests risked their lives to bring the sacraments to the faithful due to the French Revolution and the stipulations imposed on Catholics at that time.

> As a result, right from the start, John came to believe that the practice of one's beliefs was a heroic act. His instruction for his first reconciliation and first Communion took place in a

private home (1797); he celebrated his first Communion two years later and it was another two years before he was able to take Communion again. This further instilled in John the grandeur of the sacraments of reconciliation and the Eucharist.

It is said that John was naturally pious, often playing "church" with his friends when he wasn't tending his father's herds.

1802 saw an agreement being reached between Napoleon and the pope and the Catholic religion was re-established in France. John was sixteen.

1803–1813:

At the age of seventeen (1803), John became aware of his vocation to become a priest, but he could not leave his father's farm (for various reasons—the financial ones being the most frequently cited) until he was nineteen (1805), to be tutored by Father Bailey, the Curé of Ecully. He had received no education prior to this.

His schooling was a true trial as most of his fellow students were seven to eight years younger than John. He is said to have been impossible in his studies, and it is largely due to the perseverance of Father Bailey that he continued. (He truly was his spiritual guide and mentor.)

In 1809, John was drafted for military service with Napoleon's forces in Spain in error as theological students were exempt. In spite of this, John obeyed, yet he was considered to be a deserter, due to illness and the bad directions he was given to return to his unit. His brother took his place (never to return) and John was granted amnesty in 1811. John would always bear the burden of the guilt of his brother's death.

John returned to his studies with Father Bailey and, in 1812, he went to the preparatory seminary in Verrières. Not much younger than his professors, he had little success, due to his lack of Latin. With continuing perseverance, he entered the seminary in Lyons (1813), with the stipulation that he would be tutored privately by Father Bailey.

1814–1817:

After some persuasion by Father Bailey, John was allowed to take his exams in private with the Vicar General who decided that his manifest piety compensated for his lack of formal knowledge and thus, on July 2, 1814, he was ordained a subdeacon; completing his last years studies, again under the tutelage of Father Bailey.

He was ordained a deacon on June 23, 1815, and a priest on August 13 of that very same year.

His first apostolate was as an assistant to his mentor, but, because of his lack of competence in moral theology, his credentials as a confessor were not granted until several months later. He remained in this posting for three years.

John became so popular with the parishioners, because of his common-sense approach and simplistic manner, he was asked by them to be appointed rector and curate when Father Bailey died in December of 1817. But the Vicar General had other plans for him.

1818–1827:

In February 1818, the Vicar General summoned John and appointed him to a small parish of less than two hundred people in the village of Ars, some thirty miles away. He told him that "there is not much love in this village. Your job will be to instill it." This was a true challenge given to John: there remained only a few Christian families in the village due to the scourge of the Revolution—he would have to evangelize. Thus, he entered Ars, on foot, on the eve of February 9, 1818, losing his way due to the fog. Once in the village, he fell to his knees, invoked his guardian angel, and went straight to the church. What he found was discouraging, to say the least: an empty tabernacle, a tawdry altar, no steeples (revolutionaries had pulled it down), the bell hanging by a thread on questionable supports. In spite of this, Father Vianney tolled the morning Angelus bell himself that very next day.

His job would pay him five hundred francs (about one hundred dollars) a year; his presbytery had five rooms, all comfortably furnished by the Chatelaine of Ars, a noblewoman, yet John would send all of this away, keeping the barest minimum.

The new Curé was convinced that there were just two ways to convert the village: by doing penance for his villagers and by exhortation. The former was undertaken with a fervor unknown to man then and even today; he gave his bed away and slept on the damp floor (if it wasn't damp enough, he would bring water to dampen it!), using a log for a pillow, he scourged himself with an iron chain; he ate once a day (imitating that virtue of his mentor) in a minimalist manner—two or three moldy potatoes at noon, sometimes fasting for days; he got up shortly after midnight each day, went to church, and remained on his knees in prayer until Mass. His mortifications are still considered incredible to this day.

The Curé felt that there were three main evils in his parish (which he eventually said could be extended across the world to every parish): religious ignorance, pleasure seeking, and Sunday work. His job was clear-cut—he wanted to rid his parish of these scourges, which he did by condemning them forcefully from the pulpit. He also began to renovate the run-down church using his own meager funds. He drew crowds. He was controversial for his fire-and-brimstone approach, but he practiced what he preached and people converted their ways. He wept and laughed during his Masses, according to what was said. He was very proper. Within ten years, his villagers no longer stole, swore, drank excessively, worked on Sundays, or cheated in business dealings.

He undertook both the religious and secular education of the children of the village. And, since he did not believe that boys and girls should be educated together, he founded a girls' school (in 1823), choosing two young ladies from the village to be trained as teachers. In 1824, with his own money and donations, he purchased a house near the church to be used for this school.

In 1827, the success of the school was so great (as it was free), he had to establish an orphanage to handle boarders from outside the town. He ran it until 1847, when he handed it over to the Sisters of Saint Joseph. It was not a surprise that when the bishop came to visit, he found the children of Ars to be the best instructed in his diocese. John would later found a boys' school as well.

1828–1858:

Father Vianney was always available to his parishioners. He was stern in the pulpit, he fasted almost daily, mortified himself continuously, was gentle in conversation, and charitable to the poor. They say he practiced apostolic poverty. News of his holiness spread as he preached missions in nearby villages. Throughout his entire life, Father Vianney never quite understood why people came to see him. In his mind, he was an ordinary priest, preaching ordinary masses, performing his priestly duties in an ordinary manner.

Yet, there was a difference. He began to have nightly visitations by the devil. From 1824 to 1858, he had what is referred to as "manifestations," which are similar to what we now refer to being credited to poltergeists. These always came before the conversion of a particularly notorious sinner.

In 1828, the "pilgrimages" began. First, there were about twenty a day who came from neighboring areas to confess and receive Communion from Father John. The numbers increased and, from 1830 to 1859, four hundred came daily; by 1855, the crowds included religious from all over Europe. Everyone came to see him, hear him, confess to him, and receive Communion from him. It seemed that everyone was willing to wait hours, even days, to do this. Naturally, this created quite a windfall for the people of Ars: pilgrims had to be fed and accommodated for the night. Some unscrupulous individuals would gather threads from his cassocks, hair trimmings that were cut by his barber, straw from his bed and the like. For a time, it became a free-for-all until Father John put a stop to it.

His daily routine consisted of: prayer and confessions from midnight until early Mass (6:00 or 7:00 A.M.); confessions until 10:30 A.M., when he recited prime, terce, sext, and none on his knees; 11:00 A.M. saw catechism, more confessions; at noon, he ate a meager meal (if any); afternoon visits to the sick followed; vespers and compline back at the church, continuing his confessions until 7:00 or 8:00 P.M.; then, finally, rosary from the pulpit. He would then retire for his short night's rest. This was his routine, day in and day out, for more than thirty years.

Being a naturally solitary man, preferring a life of contemplation, Father John found all these pilgrims and this attention hard to take; he did try to "escape" to a monastic life of contemplation on at least three occasions, only to be forced back to Ars by the throngs of people and his sense of responsibility.

Unlike many other saints, the Curé of Ars accomplished miracles during his lifetime. The first, in 1829, involved the multiplication of a few grains of wheat into enough flour to make ten twenty-pound loaves of bread. These miracles disturbed his sense of modesty, and he always attributed them to some other saint, usually Saint Philomena, who had recently been canonized. He not only wanted to hide "his" miracles because of his own humility, he also considered that people's souls were more important than their bodies.

During the last twenty years of his life, he was afflicted with various physical illnesses of his own. Apart from wearing an iron arm band (on his left arm) that had four spikes on the inside and a hair shirt, as well as scourging himself daily, he suffered from acute neuralgia (probably from sleeping on the damp floor), he fainted often, he had violent toothaches and severe headaches. He wept at man's injustice to man when he heard confessions and became weakened from that. When he ate, it was far too little and usually spoiled food.

Also during this time, some say that he foretold dire happenings, such as World War I.

1859: In the last seven months of his life, it is reported that one hundred thousand pilgrims came to Ars. Father John was plagued with seriously ill health, often unable to speak above a whisper, subject to coughing fits. He foretold that he would die in early August of 1859.

On July 30, 1859, he went to the church, even though he was quite ill, fainting several times due to the heat; he performed his regular duties and completed his day. At 1:00 A.M. the next day, he knocked on the floor of his room, asking for the parish priest from the next village to be summoned. He was so sick that he didn't protest when they placed him on a mattress! His only complaint was when a nun tried to brush some flies away from his face saying, "leave me alone with my poor flies...sin is my only concern!" Having confessed to the parish priest, he received Viaticum at 3:00 P.M. Processions of priests carried lighted candles in procession around his deathbed—pilgrims still approached him for blessings; he had no rest, even then! He rallied and greeted the bishop at 7:00 P.M. on August 3 in a feeble voice. The bishop smiled, kissed him, and went to pray for him in the church. At 2:00 A.M. the next morning, August 4, 1859, Father John Vianney died at the age of seventy-three. He had been the Curé of Ars for more than forty-one years.

The miracles continued after his death. He was beatified on January 8, 1905, by Pope Pius X, and canonized on May 31, 1925, by Pope Pius XI. On April 29, 1929, he was designated the patron saint of all priests. For his work, he received a knighthood of the Imperial Order of the Legion of Honor by

France, into which he refused to be invested during his lifetime. The medal and insignia were, however, laid on his coffin.

It is somewhat fitting that we find that such a simple man was chosen by God to do such a complex task. All John Vianney really wanted to do was lead a contemplative life, a life that was totally dedicated to God. He wanted to spend his days in prayer, but his mission was to be something else. The will of God was to be satisfied in another way. He accepted that humbly and without question.

DAY ONE

The Lord's Work

FOCUS POINT

We are called to do the Lord's work. That is, we are called to open ourselves to God's will, to say "yes" to the divine plan. Before acting, we are to consult God in prayer. Every aspect of our lives is to begin with prayer so that we might know what is good for ourselves and for others, as well.

We are in this world, but we are not of this world seeing that we say, every day: "Our Father who art in heaven." Oh, how great it is to have a Father in heaven! "Thy kingdom come." If I let the Good God reign in my heart, he will let me reign with him in his glory. "Thy will be done." There is nothing more tender than to do the will of God, and nothing so perfect. In order to do things well, we must do them as God wants them done, in perfect conformity with his plans.

What is distinctive about the spirituality of John Vianney is the constant desire to do God's work. This extract from a commentary on the Our Father points this out. He said: "We must do things in the way that God wants them done." Yet, how do we do what God wants if we don't ask him? In order to begin to do God's work, to do his will, we must begin by stopping ourselves. Yes, stopping ourselves in all that we do in our lives: work, errands, visits, recreation.... Stop ourselves in the driving forces that set the rhythm of our daily lives. Stop ourselves in order to take time, or rather give, from time to time, give time to God, for God himself wants to take the time to meet us.

Let us be reminded of one fundamental thing: we are all sons and daughters of God, "heirs of God," through our baptism which unites us to the Father through the Son, in communion with the Holy Spirit. We are united to the Father, created in the image of the Son, in order to work in the world through the Spirit of Life. Let us be reminded that: "...we are children of God...heirs of God and joint heirs with Christ..." (Rom 8:16, 17). What good news! Let these words for life resound within us so they chase, from our spirit, any ideas of mistrust in God, as well as all ideas of predetermination in our daily lives—the time of our birth and any other element in our history.

The first book of the Bible proclaims: "God created humankind in his image, in the image of God he created them; male and female he created them" (Gen 1:27). Thus, we live a very particular relationship with the Lord, a covenant that is a gift from God and one that gives us life. We don't go to God first, he comes to us. Thus, the efforts that we can make are not destined to "win heaven" for us, but knowing that we are already participants in the divine life through the pure gift of his love, we make this reality visible through a life that is worthy of the confidence God has in us.

GOD IS LOVE

Let us begin this time of prayer with John Vianney by turning, as he did, to the One who is our Happiness, the One who, through his covenant of love, wants to work with us, in us, and through us. God's work prepares each of us, each human, to one day respond "yes" to the Life he gives us.

God is greater than we are, infinitely greater, but, at the same time, he has an intimate relationship with us. That is why he has given us the extraordinary gift of this covenant. That means that there isn't God on one side and us on the other—God is with us. Furthermore, isn't there the Christmas revelation, "Emmanuel: (meaning) God is with us"?

But just because God is with us it doesn't mean that we can do whatever we want to make him known. For our actions, our mission as baptized persons, must consist of doing God's work, like John Vianney, not works for God.

A BIG QUESTION

In fact, we have many means at our disposal to know the human and spiritual needs and expectations of mankind. There is no shortage of the number of Christian charitable organizations or those which address the developmental needs of the Third World. The number of biblical and theological courses that are open to everyone is on the rise. But a question could be asked: how is it that there are so many means at hand, so much skill, so much devotion, and yet our Church (and thus, we, ourselves) doesn't evangelize more? There is so much effort yet so few "results." Just what are we missing in the Church, and who is missing at church?

And what would we answer if God, in response, utters, "Did you consult me before acting?"

God's work is this: to begin by asking the Lord what he wants to do with me, with you, with each of us. For the Lord has a different "missionary plan" for each of us. We are not all called to be catechists, or members of a charitable organization, or to participate in a certain movement, or work in a particular service to the Church, but we must all respond to our mission as baptized believers.

Then, how do we know what the Lord wants to do with each of us? Not only for a certain choice in life, but also, and, above all, for our daily lives?

THE LORD ASKS FOR OUR "YES"

Like John Vianney, let us begin by stopping before the Lord. He said: "In order to do things well, we must do them as God wants them done, in perfect conformity with his plans." Then, in the depth of our heart, there where God is, let us say a sincere and total "yes" to the Lord. A total "yes" to let him do his work here on earth, in and through us.

> Yes, Lord, I want to do your work, your will, may you make me know it when and how you choose.

Only then will the Lord put, on our path, people who want to live according to his will. Then the Lord will send us all of the "beneficiaries" of the work that he fulfills around us, thanks to our total "yes." Isn't that what happened at Ars, as more and more penitents came to the confessional of the holy Curé?

In this way, then, before every action, and more than that, before all important undertakings, let us begin by praying. Let us have the desire to let the Lord work in us and through us. Let us ask him what is good for ourselves and others, according to his desires and will. Let us live this procedure in confidence, as did the holy Curé of Ars: no initiative of his pastoral life was made, no reply given to a delicate question, without first having prayed long about it and bringing this to the Lord.

At times, when faced with the active lives we lead, we have the tendency to say: "That's all for the monks! As lay people we don't have the time!" No, that's just it, we must stop and make the time! Strengthened with our intelligence and analytical spirit, we discover certain needs in our neighborhood or elsewhere in the world. Then, with a great desire to serve God and to offer him our work, we forget to consult him and we go off and work on our own projects and make our own plans. Often, the results are good, surely, but are they always what God wants from us, what he wants to do through us and with us?

John Vianney always relied upon the Lord, in prayer, and most particularly before the Most Blessed Sacrament, to bring all of his actions to a good end. If we let go of the One who gives us the Gospel, how can we say, "All that I do is done in the sense of the Gospel"?

God's work begins with prayer. It is often there that the Lord will "speak to our heart." But we must always discern that what we receive through prayer truly comes from the Lord, and not from our own imagination. It is here, for example, that a spiritual guide, a person who is trained in prayer and contemplation, could help us in our discernment.

In the same way, more generally, sharing with others what we experience could be a means of discernment (see Mt 18:20).

God's work, then, is to let God work in and through us. It is to want to do his work by welcoming him first into our life, as the one who holds the most important place and without whom our own "yes" has just an empty meaning. Let us hold the door of our heart open for the Lord. He is the sure guide, the light who illuminates our life. And to each of us, he shows the path which he wants us to take.

The Curé of Ars said:

Those who are led by the Holy Spirit have righteous ideas. When we are led by a strong God of light, we cannot make a mistake.... The eye of the world sees no further than a lifetime, the Christian sees to the depth of eternity.

REFLECTION QUESTIONS

Do I make prayer a regular part of my life, consulting God on every decision I make for myself and others? Do I make it a point to do God's work, to open myself to God's will as I live day to day, moment to moment? Might praying the Our Father on a regular basis—as a petition to God so that his grace and guidance will enter my life—help me to give myself over to him totally as his servant?

DAY TWO

God's Love

FOCUS POINT

We are created by Love (God); we are created to love. We are to be receptive to the love of God, a love that is available to us all. We are to accept this love of God and, in turn, share it with our brothers and sisters. We are called to read the Word of God, allow it to become a part of us, and guide us in our dealings with God and others. Just as a seed blossoms into a flower, it is right that we—as God's people—blossom into good works, works of love and compassion.

How beautiful it is to love God! My God! What would we love, then, if we didn't love (divine) Love? Man was created by Love (God), that is why he is so inclined to love. To love God with all of our heart is to love only him and make him present in all that we love.

W e must be in love to speak like this about God. And the Curé of Ars is in love with God! His logic was one of the heart, of a heart that is seduced by the revelation of God's love. In his words, we can see a proximity, a real experience of communion and communication with the Lord. Just like an extraordinary gift that he could not keep only for himself and which he wants to share with everyone, John Vianney shows us what makes him live in the very depth of himself: an immense love for this God who loves humanity.

He repeated: "To love God with all of our heart is to be ready to lose our life rather than offend him, it is to love nothing that shares our heart." Aren't those the words of a lover, filled with attention for the one who fills his heart? How many people have said this same thing to those they love?

Whoever has met with Love (God) knows how to speak with their heart. Love is not a theoretical concept. It is a vivid and life-giving experience, it is the experience of God, which the Scriptures and Tradition reveal to us. The Curé of Ars had this experience of divine love throughout his entire life and he shares it with us. Today, with him, let us love.

WHAT DOES IT MEAN, TO LOVE?

It is "to lose our life rather than offend him." It is to recognize the other person as "number one" in our life, it is to want their happiness, their true happiness. Love is beyond sentiments. It is commitment, it is the total gift of yourself to another, it is a welcome to the total gift of the other person to you. This "first place" love is the love that happens through a relationship, a knowledge of the other and the discovery of their inner beauty. It is only after the meeting and communion through the word that the meeting and the communion through the body could happen, a sign of the total and definitive covenant.

This is what we experience in the eucharistic meeting: we take communion with the Word of God before we take communion with his body. Our God is this God that is so great and beautiful who comes down to us with words of a covenant and of life, and who goes as far as shedding his blood as a testimony of the love he has for humanity, even though humanity denies him.

God is love, totally love. He is impoverished before our refusal of love. Someone who has experienced love in the context of a friendship or as a couple knows that love does not impose itself on anyone, it can't force someone's hand. If so, it isn't love. Love proposes and wants our total "yes" in order to give itself totally to our heart and to our life.

God, towards whom we go and with whom we already live, doesn't just love us with a simple courteous love, but with a love that "grabs him in the gut" and makes him say "you are my (beloved) son" (see Ps 2:7). God is impassioned with mankind, and if he holds sin in horror, it is because he knows how much it disfigures the heart and life of his children. Man was made for love. John Vianney said that man was "created for Love (God)...inclined to love."

Sin, then, is the refusal to enter into love's logic, it is to refuse God. Then, the One who is at the heart of everything, God, is pushed aside, for we take his place. By taking God's place, we center everything around ourselves, and there is a great risk of quickly seeing in someone else the one who would satisfy our desires or passions. This risk is a reality for all mankind, those who are believers, indifferent, or atheists.

The holy Curé of Ars said: "Man is poor and he needs to ask God for everything." This is a phrase that is filled with truth, for if man wants to live the meaning of love, to whom other than God could he turn to know what to do? Our world offers a thousand and one ways to live, but are all of them guided by love and respect for each other?

We are not objects to be consumed, to work and to be exploited until there is nothing left. Neither are we interchangeable, like playing pieces on the giant board game of life. Each of us is unique because we have been created in the image of God and because he wants to make his dwelling within us. That is shown in a special way at our baptism, with the water that makes us born to the trinitarian life. In the Holy Spirit, we are united to Christ who leads us to the Father.

"Do you not know that you are God's temple and that God's Spirit dwells in you? If anyone destroys God's temple, God will destroy that person. For God's temple is holy, and you are that temple" (1 Cor 3:16–17). The apostle Paul said that we are "God's temple." It is by letting God dwell in this temple that we will reveal to others what the true meaning of love is: a love that doesn't disfigure the other, but respects him in his heart, his body, and spirit; a love that makes him grow and blossom like a flower grows and blossoms when it has sunshine and water.

LOVE OPENS TO THE OTHER

For John Vianney, the love of God was not a synonym for a closed intimacy. It is the opposite of that, an opening to the other person throughout whatever may happen in our daily lives. His own life as a parish priest gives us proof of that. No matter whether he was involved in catechism, celebrations of Mass or confession, helping neighboring parish priests, or visiting with parishioners, the sick, or people passing through, the Curé of Ars "oozed" the love of God.

In the same way that Jesus didn't come to condemn but to save sinners, the holy Curé transmitted what he, himself, received from God to everyone: his merciful love for all sinners. He lived and carried the Good News everywhere, even risking being badly received and finding himself discouraged at times. But the love of God in him was "like an overflowing torrent that carries everything with it as it flows by." It's not the great mortal calm of stagnant waters, the image of a static God, but the passion of a torrent or a cascade, the image of life, action, and continual interior movement that is visible all the way to the exterior. The love of God is the image of God himself, the Holy Trinity. The Trinity is the love of the Father for the only Son through the Holy Spirit; this loving Son welcomes his Father, and, in turn, gives all his love to him through the Holy Spirit.

This love of God is also like a purifying fire that reminds each of us to tell everyone of the good path to take: it is he that we proclaim and not ourselves, it is he who leads us to eternal life and not us. Our life as Christians, then, is a testimony of love to invite all humanity to let themselves be transformed by Love (God). It is not only us who act; it is, above all, he who acts in us and through us, as long as we let him act! We are like a channel by which the Lord reveals to each human that he is loved by the trinitarian God.

The other day I was coming back from Savigneux. The birds were signing in the woods. I began to cry: poor beasts, I told myself, the Good God created you to sing and you sing. And man was made to love the Good God and he doesn't love him!

For the Curé of Ars, his concern for man traces its origins to his contemplation of God and his understanding that all men, without exception, are loved by God and capable of entering into communion with this God of love. Does man seek reasons to live? John Vianney said: "The only happiness that we have on earth is to love God and know that God loves us." Man was created for Love (God), that is the only reply, the true reply. We are created to love because we were created by the One who is love: God, the Trinity of love. Our life is God!

Then, let us allow ourselves to be loved by God, by the Father, Son, and Holy Spirit, this Trinity of love that the Church has proclaimed for over twenty centuries, a proclamation that was already prepared by all of the prophets of Israel.

John Vianney experienced the interior meeting with the Lord, and he shows us the way to it. This love of God is for us, without exception. It is for you, me, and all mankind, yesterday, today, and tomorrow, no matter what our faith and hopes are, our history, and where we live. All we have to do is open our hearts to love and let God enter to make his dwelling there, just as Jesus said in the Gospel of Saint John: "Those who love me will keep my word, and my Father will love them, and we will come to them and make our home with them" (Jn 14:23). And the Curé of Ars said: "The soul can only nourish itself with God. Only God can satisfy it, only God can fill it. Only God can satisfy its hunger."

LOVE IN PRACTICE

The Curé of Ars tells us: "We can't love God without giving him evidence of it through our works." This echoes what was said in this passage from the First Letter of Saint John, when he wrote: "We love because he first loved us. Those who say 'I love God' and hate their brothers and sisters, are liars; for those who do not love a brother or sister whom they have seen, cannot love God whom they have not seen. The commandment we have from him is this: those who love God must love their brothers and sisters also" (1 Jn 4:19–21).

It is a constant reminder to our spirit that this love for another is a visible sign of our love for God. The Curé of Ars understood it well and didn't hesitate to teach it to others. Surely, by thinking about him, we quickly have the picture in our head of a man of the Eucharist and reconciliation, but he was also a social man, one who did not hesitate to give responsibilities to his parishioners and support them in their work. We will discover this as time goes on, but if we speak of it now, it is so that our spirit doesn't become departmentalized: on the one hand, the love of God; and on the other, love for our brothers and sisters, the first being the most important. No, it isn't like that in the Christian life, and Saint John strongly reminds us of it.

As Christians, we must practice love. Often, when we hear the word "practicing Catholics," we think of the Sunday Mass. But that is to remove half of our mission as baptized believers! We are called to be "practitioners of God and others." God is the source of life who feeds us with his love, tells us what work he wants to accomplish through us, and sends us to others. We are continually sent on missions to others, each of us according to his or her particular talents and what the Lord asks us to do, according to his plan. But we don't choose between God and others. We are practitioners of the Gospel by being receivers of trinitarian love, by letting this divine life circulate in us, and by being "transmitters" of this love to those whom God sent us. John Vianney said:

The people who practice devotion, confess, and take Communion, but don't do the work of Faith and Charity, are similar to trees in bloom. You believe that there will be as much fruit as there are flowers…but there is such a great difference!

REFLECTION QUESTIONS

In what ways do I try to foster my love for God? Silent prayer before the Eucharist is an excellent way to develop this love for God. There are other ways as well, some of which are very "hands on." Might I consider involving myself in specific services that aid the poor, needy, hungry, and homeless? How might this approach, this "active prayer," benefit my desire to foster a stronger love for God? Might it help me to understand that love for God is always associated with the love I show for my brothers and sisters?

DAY THREE

Prayer

FOCUS POINT
From the very beginning, God has graced each of us with the desire to pray to him, to communicate with him. It is in the sharing that is prayer that we come to know God in a deeper way, opening our hearts to him, and seeking to know his will for us. There is a trust that is fostered in prayer, a trust that allows us to tell God everything about ourselves. It is in prayer, also, that we make requests of God, asking him for what it is we feel we need, but remaining always open to the fact that he may know better than us what we need most.

Prayer frees our souls from all material things. It lifts itself above like the fire that inflates balloons. The more we pray, the more we want to pray. It's like a fish who swims to the surface of the water, then who dives, always pushing ahead.

Time has no meaning in prayer. Prayer is nothing more than a union with God. God and the soul are like two pieces of wax that are melted together: they can't be separated. It is a very beautiful thing, this union of God with his little creature. It is a kind of happiness that we can't understand.

Having discovered what characterizes God as love, how can we not want to nourish ourselves with this love in the same way a child nourishes himself with the love and tenderness of his parents? This love is necessary for our lives, for all human life. It is offered to us so that we can live and grow in faith, hope, and fraternal love. Then a question comes to mind, a question that John Vianney often heard: "I don't know how to pray, what do I do?" The disciples had already asked this same question of Jesus, after they saw him praying: "Lord, teach us to pray…" (Lk 11:1). It is often by discovering the truth and depth of the prayer of someone else that we get the desire to learn for ourselves.

This is what the Curé of Ars replied: "It makes no difference, we don't need to speak in order to pray. We know that the Good God is there, we open our heart to him, we take pleasure in his presence, that is the best prayer." Everything is said in these two sentences. Prayer is not primarily made up of words, but of presence. The certainty of the presence of the Other, first felt in interior silence, and which then could eventually be spoken about and expressed with words.

It is not easy to pray without seeing the one who we are addressing. That is the act of faith that Jesus, himself, asks of us and encourages us to make: "Blessed are those who have not seen and yet have come to believe" (Jn 20:29); and, "I am with you always, to the end of the age" (Mt 28:20). The Lord's presence is mysterious and discreet, but very real.

God is there, present in our heart, and in our life; in the same way, we are there as well, present to his invisible presence. Prayer is a meeting of love between man and God, where God is first the "Beloved" before he is the "All-Powerful" through the strength that we often imagine. Yet, in God, the only "all-powerfulness" that exists is that of love.

This love is not a delicate love, but a jealous love for his people, a love that doesn't agree to being shared with other gods or idols. A love that knows what road leads to happiness and what road leads to sadness for his children. A love that is not resigned to see its people destroy themselves by going to false loves, false lights.

KNOW THE TRUE GOD

The Curé of Ars took pleasure in prayer. For him, it was "a tender friendship, an astonishing familiarity." It was such a good meeting place for his God that he wanted to lead all those he met to this path of life. He knew that "man is not only a working animal, he is also a spirit created in the image of God." Yet, if no one shows man the path to God, man will seek God by all kinds of paths and often run the risk of getting lost.

All we have to do is see the increasing number of persons who are interested in astrology, numerology, tarot cards, or other such "fortunetelling" sciences, as well as those who are involved in the "new age" movement: all of this reveals the religious needs that are etched in people's hearts, the need to know life and the future. This need, this search for a spiritual life, often finds itself decoyed by alluring propositions that we find marketed as being religious or esoteric, which are, in reality, false lights for man's life and true happiness.

Our mission as baptized believers is also there: for us to live the meeting with the Lord in order to be able to show the path to those around us, whether they are Christian or not. If we believe that eternal life is to know the one true God and the one he has sent, Jesus Christ (see Jn 17:3), why not begin, today, to meet the God of life, and why not show everyone this path to God, which is prayer, and treat it like a shared gift?

TRUST

Often, we are afraid. We have the impression of misunderstanding God, of misunderstanding the Bible, and of not knowing how to speak to him. It is fundamental for us to teach ourselves, to better understand our trinitarian faith in order to "always be ready to make your defense to anyone who demands from you an accounting for the hope that is in you" (1 Pet 3:15). But it is equally fundamental to believe that Christian prayer is the place of training, assured by the Lord himself. "Through prayer, we are united to God," said the Curé of Ars; we have the interior experience of the faithfulness of God and his love for mankind. God isn't a theory, he exists!

Let us not think that prayer is reserved for a select few, the monks, for example. With John Vianney, let us ask the local blacksmith, Jean-Louis Chaffangeon, what he does when he comes to church. He replies, in the local dialect, "I measure him up and he measures me up in one look." This refers to his explanation of what prayer is to him: an interior glance towards God that lets him see the weight of God's love and mercy for him. Before us, the Lord looks upon us with love and he knows us just as we are.

In prayer, God is not a judge, but rather one who gathers us to himself. Like the psalm says: "I have calmed and quieted my soul, like a weaned child with its mother; my soul is like the weaned child that is with me" (Ps 131:2). These are very human words from the Bible that allow us to better understand who God is. We will never finish discovering the Lord and being astonished by who he is. But in as much as we are not completely with him until eternity, human words can only let us express, in a somewhat acceptable manner, who the one is in whom we put our faith. The Curé of Ars didn't hesitate to explain God by using many image-laden words, as we have already seen.

To discover the proximity of the Lord is a powerful support. This is particularly true through the trials we experience in our lives. John Vianney said: "God doesn't lose sight of us in the same way as a mother doesn't lose sight of her child who is beginning to walk." Yet, quite often, we say or hear it said: "But what did I ever do to God for this to happen?" These are revealing words about how we perceive the Lord as a vengeful judge, or one who pleases himself by seeing us suffer and making us suffer....

What is important is not to determine the causes of our trials (these are generally human), but what is important is the way we live these trials. There, again, the holy Curé helps us by reminding us, following the beliefs of the Church, that trials are the places where our faith is purified by an abandonment that is even more total and trusting in the Lord. What we must do, then, in order to withstand the trials of illness, poverty, scorn, and interior worries is not to revolt against God, but get support from Jesus' prayer on the cross, when he lived his suffering in an ultimate act of trust, in spite of the impression he had of being abandoned by his Father. The Curé of Ars said:

Our crosses unite us to our Lord, they purify us, they detach us from this world, they carry the obstacles from our hearts, they help us live our lives like a bridge helps us cross a body of water.

ASK AND YOU WILL RECEIVE

In prayer, we can also ask for something. John Vianney always believed in the prayer of request, and in its effectiveness. For all prayers are granted in as much as they are moved by the love of God, others, and oneself. In as much, again, as we let God answer how he sees fit! In fact, we too often tend to tell God what he must do, how he must answer our prayers, instead of simply letting him act after we have made our request. That is why we end up begrudging God when our prayer is not answered as we had hoped, because we believe that we have not been heard. The Curé of Ars claims that if we pray with humility and trust, God answers. But, let us not forget that "tangible" answers from God are akin to signs, as if to confirm his presence amongst us. For God is neither a magician nor a vending machine! Often, his answer is spiritual, interior: a healing of the heart, a forgiveness given or received, an increase in the desire to pray or to read Scripture....

Our relationship with God is not "give and take," but based on trust and love, a relationship of love. John Vianney said: "Man does not live by bread alone, he lives by prayer, faith, adoration, and Love (God)."

REFLECTION QUESTIONS

How do I view prayer right now in my life? Do I see it as a way to better understand God and his will for my life? Do I see it as a time to spend silently in the presence of God? As an opportunity to express my gratitude to God for all the good things he has given me? Do I often petition God for specific requests during my prayer periods? If not, why not? If I do petition God during prayer, how do I verbalize my requests? Do I pray that God's will be done in all things?

DAY FOUR

The Cross

FOCUS POINT

Pain and suffering are an inevitable part of our lives. Our approach to the pain and suffering in our lives—our understanding of it, the meaning we assign to it—says so much about who we are as Christians. Jesus experienced immense physical and psychological pain and suffering during his earthly life, sanctifying suffering and making it holy as he sacrificed his life for love of us. We are called to unite our own suffering to that of Jesus' passion so that we might enter more deeply, more fully, into our relationship with the Divine.

We are such enemies with those things that are against us that we would like to live in a cushioned cocoon. It is because of suffering that we go to heaven. Illnesses, temptations, and worries are also crosses that lead us to heaven. Our Lord is a model. The cross is a ladder to heaven. How consoling it is to suffer before God's eyes and to be able to say to ourselves, at the end of our day: my soul, today you have had two or three hours of resemblance to Jesus Christ!

The cross is the inescapable passage of Christian life. Here, it is not a question of masochism, but of the reality of the spiritual life. To follow Christ is to commit oneself to follow him, to accept taking his same pathway. "If any want to become my followers, let them deny themselves and take up their cross and follow me" (Mk 8:34). For to live as a Christian is not "to live in a cushioned cocoon," said the Curé of Ars, as if to be a Christian means to be dispensed of all suffering, trials, or sicknesses. It is to take a path over which we have no control, the one of our daily lives, with its highs and lows, and on which our faithfulness to the Lord is outlined.

To live as a Christian is to accept that suffering is a part of our daily path, and thus we are able "to live" it and not submit to it. It is true that when we live through great suffering, we are thrown, at first, with respect to our regular points of reference. What appears to be necessary for our survival becomes secondary, our outlook on life changes, and a certain clarity appears. To live through suffering is to recognize our limitations, weaknesses, and human frailties. It is to turn all of this into a path of interior conversion and spiritual advancement with Christ. It is to take the way of the cross with him.

FOLLOW CHRIST

Christ's cross is obligatory for all spiritual life. Paradoxically, it is the path of love. We cannot pass directly from the Incarnation to the Resurrection. Between the two, there is the passion, the cross, and death. Jesus didn't avoid this, he even made it into a battleground and a site of victory against the forces of evil; he made it into the irreversible sign of his love for mankind and for the Father, and the sign of the love of the Father for all humanity. The cross is a scandal, for all sufferings are trials and scandals. But it is a scandal to be lived today with Christ, not turning away from him.

John Vianney, throughout his entire life, knew the trial of suffering. Whether it was moral or physical, he was not spared from it. To the contrary, he even "added" mortifications, which were part of the practices of the times. For him, it wasn't done to suffer more, but to have a greater availability for divine love and "for the sinners." This is what he said: "During the night, I suffer for the souls in purgatory and during the day for the conversion of sinners. (...) My God, grant me the favor of the conversion of my parish, I agree to suffer what you want me to throughout my life." We are already discovering, in his words, a desire for the conversion of lives through a total union with the Lord, even if he, himself, has to experience the trial of the cross. The Curé of Ars lived his trials as a means of solidarity with sinners and, by his own union with Christ on the cross, he wants to bring these sinners to discover the mercy and tenderness of God.

To follow Christ is to accept the path of the cross. By taking this path, we will discover that, along with what people think and live, proclaiming the Gospel, and practicing peace, justice, and truth are also stumbling blocks. That is where the trial of the cross begins, for the more faithful we become to

Christ, the more we make progress on the path of Christian life that is filled with the thorns of testimony.

Through experience, we know that it is difficult to live and be faithful to Christ when we are faced with people who contradict us or make fun of our faith. It is then that prayer will lead us before the cross, to the feet of the Crucified One. Jesus remained faithful to his Father to the very end, and to the proclamation of the kingdom of God offered to all people. His "yes" to the Father, his "Abba," was the revelation of his own identity as the Son, "the bread of life for mankind," leading many of his disciples to abandon him (see Jn 6:60–71). The progression of events went quickly. He was arrested, then condemned. But he never changed his path. Before the calumny, slander, sufferings, and impending death, he remained faithful to his proclamation of God's mercy for all mankind. He said, "for I have come to call not the righteous but sinners" (Mt 9:13). He let his life be crushed so that, through his own renunciation of himself out of faithfulness to the love of his Father, we would understand the immensity of his love for us.

THE CROSS LEADS
TO HIGH ACHIEVEMENT

Through prayer and the contemplation of Christ on the cross, we grow in our faith. The trials that we experience are no longer felt to be barriers that cut us off from God, but are lived as a path of purification for our hearts, leading us to a total abandonment of ourselves into the hands of the Lord. It is the acceptance of our own limitations and weaknesses, not something to be "coped with" as best we can, but rather to recognize the greatness of the Lord, to let him transform our lives in order to make them become the living words of God for today.

To go beyond our limitations and sufferings starts with our acceptance of the agonizing struggle that it provokes in us. For example, the struggle between the work that needs to be done and what we are able to do, between the fact that we want to proclaim Christ and what we actually proclaim, between the desire to be active and the illness that forces us to bed.

This higher achievement, then, is experienced in interior peace, through a total abandonment of our life to the hands of God. But do not think that this will be easy. At times, it will take a long process to reach that point. John Vianney, himself, said: "We must have already reached a certain degree of perfection in order to withstand illness with patience." It is necessary, however, to want to grow in this way, even if, at first, we are revolted by interior or physical suffering. We must desire to experience this unity with Christ on the cross, and ask him to make our faith grow in us. Let us again hear what the Curé of Ars said: "Whether we want to or not, we must suffer. There are those who suffer like the good thief, others like the bad one. Both suffer equally. But one of them knows how to make his sufferings meritorious. He accepts them in a spirit of repentance, turning to the crucified Jesus, he received these beautiful words from his mouth: 'Today, you will be with me in paradise.'"

THE BOOK OF THE CROSS

The cross of Jesus was always a scandal. To believe in Jesus, yes, but to believe that we are saved by the cross, that's foolish! A God of love, yes, but a God who dies on a cross, no! From the beginning of the Church, Christ's disciples had been confronted with a great deal of mockery. The apostle Paul alludes to it in his first letter to the Corinthians: "but we proclaim Christ crucified, a stumbling block to Jews and foolishness to Gentiles, but to those who are the called (the chosen ones), both Jews and Greeks, Christ (is) the power of God and the wisdom of God" (1 Cor 1:23–24). In his own way, full of images, John Vianney, made comparisons with the cross: "The cross is the key that opens the door, the lamp that illuminates heaven and earth, it is the ladder to heaven. The cross is the wisest book we could read; those who don't know this book are ignorant."

By the cross, we are freed from sin—this sin that is a refusal of God and leads to the interior destruction of mankind. Within us, sin brings about a distancing from God, making us weak with respect to our human and spiritual behavior. On the cross, God assumes the sins of man and destroys them. God is the vanquisher of sin through the pardon he gives to mankind. "On behalf of Christ, be reconciled to God" (2 Cor 5:20). At the heart of sin, the cross is like a door opened by God, letting flow the light of reconciliation that gives life to our bodies which have already been marked by death.

To welcome the cross into our life is to draw from it the strength that goes beyond our weaknesses and, through it, to enter into the light of life. The spiritual remedy for the sufferings we experience is not found in books or in distractions, but in the cross. It is by associating ourselves to the passion of Christ, by uniting ourselves to him that we can hold on. We believe that the cross is not the end, it is the "ladder to heaven," the path that leads to resurrection and the meeting with the Father. We believe that Christ conquered suffering and death. Through our faith in him, our "adaptation" to him and with him, we can live each day of trial as a spiritual battle against evil, with the hope, one day, of entering into the bounty of the resurrection of Christ, "the firstborn from the dead" (Col 1:18).

REFLECTION QUESTIONS

How do I approach pain and suffering in my own life? Am I conscious of the fact that through his Incarnation, passion, and death, Jesus Christ made holy all aspects (including suffering) of the human experience? Am I able to see that even in the midst of pain and suffering (a mode of being which can cause one to focus only on one's own affliction), God is present and is calling me to greater depths in my relationship with him?

DAY FIVE

The Eucharist

FOCUS POINT

God is fully present in the Blessed Sacrament, the Eucharist, the body and blood of Jesus Christ. We are called to receive our Lord in the Eucharist frequently, just as John Vianney called his parishioners to do. We come to know our Lord to great depths through the sacrament of holy Communion, in which we are nourished by the gifts and grace of our God. We are called to foster a deep devotion to the Blessed Sacrament in our spiritual lives, our desire to do so coming from the One who loved us into creation.

After the consecration, the Good God is there just as he is in heaven. How beautiful! If man knew this mystery well, he would die of love; God spares us because of our weakness. When God wanted to nourish our souls to support them

throughout life, he cast his glance on creation and found noth-
ing worthy of it. Then, he turned it on himself and decided to
give himself. O my soul! How great you are since only God
can satisfy you! The food for the soul is the body and blood of
God! Oh, beautiful food! That is something, if we think about
it, to lose oneself for eternity in this abyss of love!

For the Curé of Ars, the Eucharist was first and foremost the experience of the meeting, the meeting with the One who gave his life as food for the multitude, the One who gave his life so that mankind would have life in its plenitude. The Eucharist, and more precisely, communion with the body and blood of Christ, is a meeting with the living God, a covenant that he seals with us and we seal with him, a covenant that is renewed and reaffirmed each time we receive Communion.

THE TOTAL AND DEFINITIVE COVENANT

On the evening of Holy Thursday, when Jesus celebrated Passover with his disciples, he transformed this meal that was a sign of the passage of the Hebrew people from slavery in Egypt to the freedom of the Promised Land. He made it into a meal that would become the sign of the passage from the slavery of sin and death to the freedom of life. Into the bread offered to the Father in heaven, and given to the apostles, Jesus came to "enclose" his life and his entire being to make it become his body, to make it the sign of his presence; a new and eternal covenant, total and definitive, that nothing can equal other than meeting with the Lord himself when he will come to take us with him.

In this bread and wine offered at the eucharistic table, the Church always recognized the sign of the real presence of the living Christ. For John Vianney, this faith in the real presence is truly an experience of God's covenant with mankind: "How tender and consoling are the thoughts of the holy Presence of God.... If we have faith, we would see Jesus Christ in the Sacrament." Yes, it is Christ there, waiting for us, the one who continuously prays to the Father for us. It is a covenant for life that is sealed by Christ in the Eucharist. A covenant with God who, instead of resigning himself to our breaking the covenant, comes continuously to meet us in order to offer his love and to renew the bond with humanity that nothing could destroy. In the Eucharist, God definitively gives himself to mankind.

As baptized believers, we are the first beneficiaries of this covenant of love. But do we always understand this gift from God? The holy Curé said: "We have too much happiness. We will only understand it in heaven, how sad that is!" In fact, each time that we receive the Eucharist, we enter into the greatest communion that is possible to experience with the Lord on earth—simply because it was not man who invented the Eucharist to unite him with God, but God himself who gave it to his people! And it is God who invited mankind to nourish himself with him. Jesus said: "no one has greater love than this, to lay down one's life for one's friends" (Jn 15:13), and the greatest gift that God gave us is himself. In Communion, it is God, himself, that comes to dwell in us.

HE IS THERE!

"He is there...he is there!" How many times John Vianney said these words when he showed the tabernacle to everyone! Quite often, in his preaching or catechism, he came back to the Eucharist, the presence of God in the midst of his people. His preaching turned the hearts of people towards the real presence of the Lord: "He is there in the sacrament of his love," he said. To support his words, he had a little pulpit built, one that permitted him to be able to see both the faithful and the holy Sacrament simultaneously. The goal of his preaching was to make people aware of the eucharistic presence. This conviction motivated him, even before the Church did, to invite Christians to take Communion frequently. If the Eucharist is, in reality, the gift that God makes of himself to mankind, why should people deprive themselves of it? In the same way as our bodies need food to live, so does our faith. The consecrated bread and wine are the true food and drink which our spiritual lives need.

The Word of the Lord is the first food for our faith, but this Word leads us to want a covenant that is more total with the Lord. Not a fusion with God, but a loving meeting in the "otherness" of persons. Yet, for our time on earth, the Lord gives us food for the journey: the Bread of Life. "I am the bread of life…very truly, I tell you, unless you eat the flesh of the Son of Man and drink his blood, you have no life in you…those who eat my flesh and drink my blood abide in me, and I in them" (Jn 6:35, 53, 56).

When we celebrate the Eucharist, we live a dual relationship with the Lord: him and me, me and him. Mass is both this movement where man offers himself to God and intercedes for all his brothers and sisters, but also this movement where God gives himself as food for mankind. We have the chance, in the eucharistic celebration, to live in proximity with the Lord; one more reason to bring into our prayers those who are not present. The celebration is a missionary action where each of us takes care of his brothers and sisters. And furthermore, like the Curé of Ars, we will come to have the conviction of the real presence of God in our celebrations, and we will want to make others around us aware of this joy of meeting with the One who is the Life for all humanity. For the Eucharist is not reserved for just a select few; it is God's gift to all humanity, and through him, to all creation.

To signify the greatness of this sacrament, John Vianney kept watch over the quality of the celebrations: Masses, processions.... He knew that one single liturgy could convert someone who was there. But quality doesn't mean a spectacle with an abundance of gold, incense, and music. For him, the source of the quality of his celebrations was found in the interior life of the one who celebrated them. That is why he prepared himself for the celebration of the Eucharist by a long time of adoration. Nothing and no one could hinder this time. It was the same for the participants: an assembly is the sign of the presence of Christ in as much as they adhere, interiorly, to what is celebrated. Therefore, their exterior behavior would be modified, transformed; that is, particularly, through the quality of our faith and our assemblies where we give witness. The Curé of Ars said it thus, in his own way: "What could one think when we see the manner in which the majority of Christians behave in our churches? Some think of their temporal affairs, others about their pleasures; this one is asleep, and that one finds the time long; one turns his head, another yawns, one scratches himself, one thumbs through his book, and yet another looks to see if it will all soon be over with."

ADORATION

To be loved and to love is the most profound desire that could be etched into the heart of each person—love that finds its fullness in its fulfillment in the union with God, the source of all love. God is love, and mankind has a thirst for the living God. John Vianney said: "The earth is too small to offer something that could satisfy the soul: it thirsts for God. Only God could satisfy it."

If Communion is a powerful stimulant for our faith, adoration is the preparation for the eucharistic meeting, as well as a prolongation of it. To adore the Lord in the Bread of Life is to recognize that he is there, not only when we want to meet him during a celebration, but continuously, not needing our desire in order to exist. Christ is there always. He is present in the host, independent of our will. His presence is the sign of the Father's faithfulness to the covenant sealed for all time with mankind through the death and resurrection of the Son.

To adore the Lord is to recognize that he is the All-Powerful, that there is a distance between him and me, a distance that permits communication. Adoration draws our gaze to Christ, "decenters" us from ourselves and the judgment that we make about ourselves in order to contemplate the One who is the Resurrection and the Life. It cuts off all impressions we could have about ourselves. It centers us on what is important, Christ, the Son of God, who leads us to the Father, through the Holy Spirit he gave us. For Christ the Lord is greater than we are. By coming to meet him in adoration and recognizing ourselves as sinners, we allow him to shine a ray of his light towards us and prepare us for the sacrament of reconciliation.

"And by this we know we are from the truth and will reassure our hearts before him, whenever our hearts condemn us; for God is greater than our hearts, and he knows everything" (1 Jn 3:19–20). Through his eucharistic presence, the Lord reminds us that he is the watchman, the one who knocks at the door of our heart and waits. Our future in the covenant of love and mercy that the Lord comes to live with us depends only on our total "yes," true and durable, given freely and in confidence.

REFLECTION QUESTIONS

In what ways do I foster a devotion to the Blessed Sacrament in my spiritual life? Might I pray before the tabernacle before or after Mass to increase my devotion? Might I consider becoming a daily communicant for a period of time? Perhaps spiritual reading that specifically addresses devotion to the Blessed Sacrament might be beneficial to my spiritual life. Might I consult a priest, religious, or spiritual director as to what books would best suit this desire to deepen my spiritual life?

DAY SIX

Reconciliation

FOCUS POINT

God calls us to the sacrament of reconciliation because he loves us so much, wants to forgive us, wants his relationship with us to be without the obstacle of sin. When we choose less than God, we sin. But God pursues us despite our failings—his mercy is beyond our understanding. He loved us into creation, and loves us forever after. Sin cannot stop his love. Let us participate in the sacrament of reconciliation regularly so that there will be no obstacles between ourselves and God.

If the sinner goes further astray, this tender Father does not stop offering him his forgiveness. It isn't the sinner who comes back to God to ask for forgiveness for himself, but it is God, himself, who runs after the sinner and makes him come back to him. His greatest pleasure is to forgive us.... Our sins are

*grains of sand next to the great mountain of God's mercies....
How great is God's bounty: his good heart is an ocean of mercy;
such great sinners that we could be never have to despair about
our salvation. It is so easy to save oneself!*

———

Forgiveness is the greatest proof of love and trust we can
bring to someone who has hurt us. To love is to go all the
way to forgiveness. Nothing is more difficult than forgiveness,
for it is not forgetting, but a recognition of the reality that was
experienced and a renewal of the other through trust expressed.
Through forgiveness, the sin committed can no longer be re-
called in the least outburst, but is experienced like a transfer to
the past of an event that will not have any further effect on the
current or future relationship with the other person. The forgiveness given is like a resurrection experienced by the other
which allows a common future to occur.

To forgive is not to say: "I forgive you, we'll act as if nothing has happened"; nor is it to say, "I forgive you, but the next
time I will penalize you." To truly live forgiveness is to live a
dual event. The person who hurts me recognizes that his action has broken off our relationship, and I, myself, recognize
that there was a wound in me that brings a rupture of trust
along with it. To reconcile with the other person is to show
that what binds us together is stronger than the hurt committed and that, through love, it is forgiven. Forgiveness is an act
of faith, hope, and extraordinary trust in the other person. It is
God dwelling in us each time we go to receive the sacrament
of love, the sacrament of God's infinite mercy for each of us.

TO RECOGNIZE OURSELVES AS LOVED

To recognize ourselves as sinners, we must recognize the sin committed and the wound caused to the other person. But if we can confess our sin, we are already recognizing that the love God has for us is greater than our sin. God is love, totally love. Our Christian life consists of practicing the love of God within us and around us. Sin is a lack of love, it is to turn away from the road that Christ cleared for us, it is to no longer fully be the sign of God's covenant for our brothers and sisters. Concretely, it is to be stained by pride, egoism, self-importance, scorn, aggressiveness, self-profit.... Nevertheless, God loves us, in spite of our sins. It is like this father who impatiently awaits the return of his prodigal child and who, right from the time he sees him, runs to throw himself into his arms (see Lk 15:11–32). Like the Curé of Ars said, God "runs after the sinner," not to punish or condemn him, but because he loves him and it tears him apart to see his child so far off the road of life.

God is love, and it is when we see such a love he has given us, brought to us, that we recognize our sins. Before such love, nothing can justify one sin or another. No argument holds before divine love to minimize our responsibility and our lack of love. For the love of God is a love that is close at hand, lived through a total commitment, and not a love of condescension that could not be attained. This proximity is truly signified by the covenant in Christ. God makes a total commitment of himself to humanity and signs it with the blood of the cross.

God is not only the one who created us one day and gives us an appointment at the end of time to make an accounting of our sins and decide our destiny. The God of the covenant sealed in Jesus Christ is this God who gives himself continuously to man so that he lives, for without God, without love, man could not live. And if man breaks the covenant along this path, God leaves to seek him. He asked Adam, "where are you?" (Gen 3:9). God does not resign himself to accept our ruptures of the covenant. He did not create us to let us go to our demise, for he knows that sin overwhelms man. His greatest desire is to see us come back to him and sin no more.

But let us be careful to not disfigure this divine love by saying to ourselves: "anyway, God forgives." God doesn't act like that. If God forgives, it is because he loves us. Then, let us be sincere in our requests for forgiveness, and let us be sorry for our sins. But if we fall back into sin, let us not resign ourselves to that, for the Lord knows and wants us to be greater than our sins. Let us always have an awareness, honed by love, that the greatest proof of God's trust in us is his forgiveness.

EXPRESSING OUR SIN

During the actual act of the sacrament of reconciliation, there is the time when we accept our sins. It is not the most important time, for that is forgiveness. But, without a doubt, it is the most difficult, for it forces us to see what we are: sinners. The most trying time is when we have to express our sin before a priest. Before we go any further, let us listen to the holy Curé: "I know that the confession of your sins causes you a moment of humiliation. Is it really humiliating to confess your sins? The priest knows, more or less, what you may have done. I am much guiltier than you: don't be afraid to confess...."

The things that permit us to be in a relationship with another person are our words, gestures, and behavior. It is by speaking to someone that we can get to know them. The act of speaking permits us to be aware of and make sense of what we are thinking. Thus, through speech, we put a distance between what is said and ourselves. What is expressed comes from us and, at the same time, no longer belongs to us, since it has left our mouth. It is like that for the recognition of our sins. To express them signifies that we have gotten control of them in our conscience, that we accept them as they are. But so that we can separate them from ourselves, to put some distance between us and them, we must make them leave by the means of speech. Speech allows us to put some distance between us and our sins, which thought cannot do. Thus, expressed and recognized, John Vianney said: "at the moment of absolution, the Good God throws our sins over his shoulder, that is, he destroys them. They will never reappear. The sins that we hide will all reappear. In order to hide them well, we must confess them."

WELCOMING FORGIVENESS

In the sacrament of reconciliation, God affirms his forgiveness in our life. It is the rupture of this infernal circle of sin in which we are often caught. Forgiveness is like a resurrection of the person, it is an experience of the active presence of God in the heart of our life. It is the renewal of our baptism, which, one day, united us definitively with the Father, Son, and Holy Spirit, and made us "carriers of God" to the heart of the world.

The words of absolution from the priest don't come from him. It is in the name of the Lord that he forgives, by reason of the mission with which the Church has entrusted him. Knowing that we don't pardon ourselves, let us discover just how important it is to hear the priest tell us the words of life. In the same way that it is vital to express what hinders us on the path of God, it is as vital to hear the Lord express his mercy through the ministry of the priest. "I will give my ministers the responsibility to proclaim, to mankind, that I am always ready to receive them, that my mercy is infinite," said the Curé of Ars, speaking in the name of the Lord.

For God is not a judge, but a Father who wants to give happiness to mankind. His forgiveness is a source of peace, truth, and interior healing. Each person is loved for themselves and forgiven by God. God doesn't pardon us "in general," but he wants to manifest a unique love to each one of us, for each of us is personally known by the Lord, each of us is unique to him.

And if we happen to hear the Curé of Ars speaking about hell, let us not believe that it is something outdated. "Hell has its origins in the goodness of God," he said. For what is hell if it isn't the possibility open to mankind, who was created free and responsible for himself, to refuse to the end, in all conscience and clarity, the love of God? Hell is the "place" of non-love par excellence, "where it will be very painful to be separated from God," said John Vianney.

No one could say if there is anyone in hell, but if we believe that God loves us with a profoundly respectful love, wanting us to be free and responsible for our actions, we must say, at the same time, that God could not force us to live with him for eternity. Love does not force itself on anyone, it is offered— even all the way to running the risk of being refused.

I love you, O my God, and I only fear hell because we will never have the tender consolation of loving you there.

REFLECTION QUESTIONS

How often do I participate in the sacrament of reconciliation? If I do not go to confession regularly, why not? What are those fears or issues that prevent me from welcoming God's forgiveness into my life through this sacrament? Might speaking with a priest, religious, or spiritual director benefit me if I am struggling with making the sacrament of reconciliation a regular part of my spiritual life? How does my understanding of this sacrament affect my willingness and desire to forgive those people in my own life who have wronged me in some way?

DAY SEVEN

With Mary

FOCUS POINT

It is Mary's lifelong "yes" to God that we try to imitate in our own lives. Mary gave herself totally over to God's will; we are called to do the same. There is no doubt that in our attempts to do so, we will faces obstacles, temptations, and difficulties. When we encounter such areas of concern, we must call out to the Blessed Virgin Mary, and ask that she intercede on our behalf to the Father, securing his graces for our benefit. We can have no greater advocate that Mary in this regard, she who delivered God incarnate from her very womb.

The Father enjoys seeing the Blessed Virgin as the ultimate masterpiece created by his own hands. The heart of this good mother is nothing but love and mercy. She only wants to see us happy. All we have to do is turn to her to be answered. The more we are sinners, the more tenderness and compassion she has for us. We don't go into a house without speaking to the doorkeeper. So, the Blessed Virgin is the doorkeeper of heaven.

T he Curé of Ars said: "I loved her even before I knew her. She is my oldest love." It is true that when we look at the life of John Vianney, we quickly discover the presence of Mary. From the beginning to the very end, she was there, discreet but always present in his heart.

DISCREET PRESENCE

It is the same with the Gospels, the presence of Mary is almost secondary in the life of the Curé of Ars. She is his companion, the one who leads him to the Lord, but she never holds the most important place. She is there in the Gospels, present for the important events: the Annunciation, the Visitation, the Nativity, Cana, the crucifixion, and the Resurrection. For each event, she is the "teacher" for our faith through her behavior or her words. Her "yes" that is constant and trusting in the will of the Father is a lesson, support and encouragement for the disciple of the past as well as of today. Using a minimum of words and gestures, she teaches us what is important. She simply leads us to her son. Nothing makes her the center of attention, but through her, our glance and behavior find themselves oriented towards the Lord.

With respect to the apparitions that the Curé of Ars experienced, he remained discreet. He never denied them, but he made no further comments about them either. As did the Mother of God, he preferred to speak about the Lord rather than himself—a behavior that is a complete education for us. For the only glory that we have to seek is that of the Lord and not our own, by whatever means possible.

On the other hand, John Vianney speaks to us of the Blessed Virgin with a great deal of confidence. He speaks of her as someone he knows well, and presents her mostly as someone who is close to the Holy Trinity: "The three divine Persons contemplate the Blessed Virgin." Finally, she is the one to whom we can ask anything and everything: "When our hands have touched herbs, they perfume all that they touch. Let us pass our prayers through the hands of the Blessed Virgin, she will perfume them!"

THE IMMACULATE CONCEPTION

On the subject of the proclamation of the dogma associated with the Immaculate Conception, in 1854, John Vianney said: "What happiness! I always thought that the Catholic truths were always lacking this ray of light. It is a gap that cannot remain in religion." For quite a while, he loved speaking about Mary, who was conceived without sin. On May 1, 1836, almost twenty years before the pontifical proclamation, he consecrated his parish to Mary, conceived without sin.

Mary was all purity, the one who was filled with grace, "favored" according to the words of the angel on the day of the Annunciation (see Lk 1:28). In her, there were no traces of sin, and that was because of the pure grace of the Lord. At the very moment of her conception, Mary was already entrusted with the bounty of the Holy Spirit. This does not signify a "setting apart" of the Virgin from the world of the sinner, but rather a preparation for the maternity that would, one day, be proposed to her.

Mary would not become any less free, just to the contrary, for freedom is the interior capacity of the human being to choose what is good for him with respect to his divine filiation, and thus respond positively to the will of God. The foundation of freedom is to say "yes" to God and his love, and this foundation traces its source to the heart of mankind and not to the rules of life in a society.

Mary's immaculate conception was not given free of trials. Like us, she experienced moments of conflict, and even temptations. Thus, we read the following in the Gospel of Mark: "Then his (Jesus') mother and his brothers came; and standing outside, they sent to him and called him. A crowd was sitting around him; and they said to him, 'Your mother and your brothers and sisters are outside, asking for you.' And he replied, 'Who are my mother and my brothers?' And looking at those who sat around him, he said, 'Here are my mother and my brothers! Whoever does the will of my God is my brother and sister and mother'" (3:31–35). This was an event that was difficult for Mary to live through who, for a moment, was questioning herself about her son. But if there may have been the temptation to strike Jesus, there was no sin. And the son led the mother back to the first step of her mission—the total "yes" to God. She was fully his mother because she did the will of God. When we have a difficult time discerning the will of God for our life, let us pray to the Blessed Virgin to support us and lead us to the whole truth.

MARY, THE MOTHER OF THE CHURCH

Mary is a gift from God to the Church. She is given to us as the one who, with and for us, intercedes with her son. Thus, in Cana, she acted as an intermediary between the wedding servers and Jesus. She was there, present. Few words were necessary, no discussion.

At the foot of the cross, she said nothing. It was Jesus who, in a few words, gave his mother to the Church, through the apostle John. The Curé of Ars comments on this passage by saying: "Jesus Christ, after having given all that he could give us, wanted to again make us heirs of what he held to be most precious, that is, his holy Mother."

The apostles were the pillars of Christ's Church, Christ being the cornerstone. On them rests the proclamation of the Good News of the Resurrection. On them, the Church, the people of God, the Body of Christ, and the Temple of the Holy Spirit support themselves. John is the "beloved" disciple, he is also the one who remained, right to the end, close to Jesus, in his passion and death on the cross. In the same way, Mary, always a discreet presence, was there, with John. It was then that Jesus said, "Woman, here is your son"; then he said to the disciple, "Here is your mother" (Jn 19:26, 27). That was much more than simple concern for assuring the material future of Mary. What we have here is a spiritual gift. The one who received the Word of God in her womb now receives the Body of her son, the Church. And the apostle John, the symbol of the burgeoning Church, received Mary as a precious treasure, as the Mother of God.

Mary is not "the fourth Person in the Holy Trinity," nor the one who places herself between God and mankind. We don't adore Mary, but we can pray to her, for she is the one who said "yes" to God and teaches us to say "yes"; she is the one who let God do his work in her and teaches us the same; she is the one who knows God so well that she teaches us, by her life, to want to make our life an expression of "I love you, God." She is the Mother of God, for Jesus is God, the only Son of God.

John Vianney said: "I think that, at the end of the world, the Virgin Mary will be very quiet, but as long as the world exists, we tug at her from all sides...." Yes, until the end of time, through her, we can address our prayer to the Lord, and ask her to pray for us, for each of us needs prayer to grow in faith, especially when trials touch us. May Mary, at the foot of the cross, help us to live our own crosses in faith. "Holy Mary, Mother of God, pray for us poor sinners...."

REFLECTION QUESTIONS
Have I fostered a strong devotion to the Blessed Virgin in my life? What types of spiritual reading might benefit me in fostering such a devotion? Have I considered praying the rosary on a regular basis? What areas of my life do I continue to close off from God's love? How might a stronger devotion to Mary make my entire life a "yes" to the will of God, and a commitment to serve him in everything I do and say? I must never forget the love Mary has for creation—and me personally—and her willingness and desire to intercede on my behalf.

DAY EIGHT

Community Sharing

FOCUS POINT

As members of the Church, the Body of Christ, we are parts of a whole. Our Head is Jesus Christ, and he has given us the Holy Spirit to guide us in our pilgrimage as God's Church on earth. We are social people, the people of God, and we interact with one another, supporting each other through difficult times, allowing God's love to shine through us as we serve each other according to the Gospel model. By sharing our unique experience of God with each other, we come to a greater understanding of our creator, his varied graces, and his immense love for his creation.

The Holy Spirit is our leader. Man is nothing by himself, but he is a great deal with the Holy Spirit. Man is all earthly and all animal. Only the Holy Spirit can lift his soul and carry it to heaven. Those who are led by the Holy Spirit have righteous ideas. That is why there are so many ignorant people who know more than the scholars.

J ohn Vianney didn't hesitate sharing, with those close to him, what he experienced with the Lord and what he discerned of the action of God around him. This was particularly true with his vicar, the missionaries, and the Brothers of the Holy Family in Belley who accompanied him in his ministry in Ars during the final years of his life.

It was also a sharing in the Holy Spirit, for without the Holy Spirit, we can't see God at work in and around us. "Only the Holy Spirit can lift our soul and carry it to heaven." The Holy Spirit opens us to God, it "magnifies our outlook, just as eyeglasses magnify objects," explained the Curé of Ars.

LIKE THE FIRST CHRISTIANS
Easily in conversation, with others, we share what we are living, our impressions about one event or another. In a certain way, we are telling it to ourselves. Sharing in the Holy Spirit, or communal sharing, consists of telling others we meet, not only about what we experience, but mostly how we see God present in one or another event in our life. That is what the Curé of Ars experienced every time he spoke of his meetings with the parishioners, pilgrims, or on the subject of the free school (the *Providence*). It is a method of sharing that we already find in the Acts of the Apostles: "When they arrived, they called the church together and related all that God had done with them, and how he had opened a door of faith for the Gentiles" (Acts 14:27).

It is the Holy Spirit who allows us to discern and give witness to all that God does through us. What the first Christians experienced is not something that happened only in the past. In shared experiences there is a call sent to the Church of all eras. In fact, what makes faith grow is not only knowledge of the Scriptures and the personal experience of God, but also the sharing of what each of us experiences with the Lord, and how we see him act. This type of sharing makes us discover that God doesn't only act through a particular person, he acts through each of us, in a different way at times, but never in a conflicting manner.

The Holy Spirit was given to all of us. In the Acts of the Apostles, we even see that it came before the apostles' proclamation of the Gospel. That is the case in the story of Peter and Cornelius, the centurion in chapter ten of the Acts of the Apostles, where the latter was filled with the Holy Spirit even before he was baptized. But it is the end of this story that is of interest to us in our day of prayer on the theme of communal sharing: it is through the sharing of what Peter experienced and how he saw God at work that the community of Jerusalem recognized that God had really acted, and in turn, gave thanks to the Lord. "When they heard this, they were silenced [of their criticisms]. And they praised God, saying, 'Then God has given even to the Gentiles the repentance that leads to life'" (Acts 11:18).

GOD PRESENT AT THE HEART OF OUR LIVES

The Curé of Ars said: "Those who are led by the Holy Spirit have righteous ideas." The One who allows us to "see" God present among us is the Holy Spirit. Again, we must want to be inhabited by the Holy Spirit! At times, we have so many

preconceived ideas about God and about the way he acts that
we have a great deal of difficulty seeing him at work today in
us, next to us, or through others. That is what John Vianney
meant when he spoke of ignorant people and scholars. That is
what Jesus said after having heard the seventy disciples joy-
fully tell him what they had done in his name: "...Father, Lord
of heaven and earth, because you have hidden these things
from the wise and the intelligent and have revealed them to
the infants..." (Lk 10:21).

Christ's joy comes following the disciple's sharing of their
lives. It was under the action of the Holy Spirit that he was
filled with joy and proclaimed this prayer of praise. It is this
kind of communal sharing that we can experience in the
Church.

To tell each other how we see the Lord at work today in
us, through us, and around us, is to give a fresh breath of life
to our faith. It is also to marvel at the action of God through
the Holy Spirit, an action with many expressions. To share in
this way also permits us to not "enclose" God through our
single gaze and reduce him to what we are. God is greater than
we are. We experience this each time we share these events,
with our brothers and sisters, where we see the Lord at work.
For us, this then becomes a source of praise and joy.

SHARING AND PRAYING

In order to become aware of the active presence of God in
him, through him, and around him, the Curé of Ars didn't
have any particular technique. He simply prayed and now in-
vites us to pray: "Each morning, we must say: 'My God, send
me your Holy Spirit, so that he will make me know what I am
and what you are.'"

It is by having both our eyes and heart turned to the Lord that, little by little, we can learn to "discover," in our world and our life, the signs of his presence. For the true prayer is not one that makes us flee from the world, but one which leads us to see God in the world. The world is not to be rejected, but to be loved, for God loved it first and wants to lead it to its full blossoming, through the covenant of eternal life. If there is sin in the world, we must not flee the world, for sin belongs to us. The more we truly pray to the Lord, the more we will learn to see him present today, and, at the same time, the more we will discover how far we are, at times, from living according to his will. Far from leading us to pride and the feeling that we have already arrived in heaven, prayer and communal sharing teach us humility and poverty of heart.

Thus, to meet the Lord in prayer and see the signs of his presence in our world, calls for us to have wonder in our hearts. We who are so little before God our Father, we become his adoptive children through Christ (see Rom 8:15 and Eph 1:5).

Communal sharing makes us grow in faith and teaches us to speak about God to those people we know. This verbal form of witness is engaging, for through it, we "speak God" to others. Let us ask the Lord to show us the signs of his presence and teach us to learn to experience true communal sharing, not to "impress" others, but so we take the opportunity to speak about these signs, give witness, so that, in this way, each of us can grow in our faith in the living and active God.

REFLECTION QUESTIONS
How active am I as a member of the Church, of my parish, or my community? Do I feel called to do more as a member of the Body of Christ? If I do indeed hear God calling me to a more

active role in the Church, what area of service might suit my particular God-given talents? Do I enjoy working with people "one on one"? Am I called to lead a group devoted to working for a specific goal? If I am not so much of a "people person," there are many other ways I can get involved in service to the Church. Might I consider talking with my pastor, director of religious education, or the various people who make up my parish council about a way of service that appeals to me?

DAY NINE

The Welcome We Have for Others

FOCUS POINT

As Christians, we must never hesitate to leave God for God. If we are in prayer, and a neighbor in need calls out to us, we should not feel burdened to leave our prayer to God so as to address service to God and love of God by aiding our neighbor. We must always be at the ready to show God's love to others when we see them in need. We are called to go outside of ourselves, to express our love for God and neighbor in concrete, practical ways. Whether it be "hands on" assistance or donating clothes or money to charity, God calls us to give to others as he has given to us.

There are those who say to the poor that they seem to look to be in such good health: "You are so lazy! You could work. You are young. You have strong arms." You don't know that it is God's pleasure for this poor person to go to you and ask for a handout. You show yourself as speaking against the will of God. There are some who say: "Oh, how badly he uses it!" May he do whatever he wants with it! The poor will be judged on the use they have made of your alms, and you will be judged on the very alms that you could have given but haven't.

D uring the entire life of John Vianney, from his birth to his death, the poor occupied an important place. They were offered a special welcome in his family home. The Vianney family was known for their hospitality and practice of charity. Oftentimes, there were more than ten poor people at their supper table. And if they ran out of soup, John's father would give them his. The farm buildings also served as accommodations for those who had no other place to go for the night. "Ordinarily, they would put up quite a few there, up to twenty people at a time," wrote Catherine Lassagne, citing the holy Curé.

Knowing this, we are not surprised to hear the Curé of Ars speak to us about caring for the underprivileged and see him practice this "ministry to the poorest" himself with such great love. But if he did so, it was not simply because he had seen his parents do this when he was a child, it was because there was a pressing evangelical calling. In this manner, our love for God is translated to our brothers and sisters, in particular the most underprivileged, in a concrete manner. It is a love that is experienced without a fuss, in the silence of the heart: "But when you give alms, do not let your left hand know what your right hand is doing, so that your alms may be done in secret; and your Father who sees in secret will reward you" (Mt 6:3–4).

GOD IN THE POOR

The Curé of Ars said: "You must never scorn the poor, for this scorn falls onto God. Often, we believe that we are helping a poor person and it turns out that it's our Lord." Faithful to the Bible and the Tradition of the Church, John Vianney created a strong connection between the poor and God. God is always perceived as being the one who is close to the little ones, the poor, the weak, and the oppressed. For in each person, God is present, and to leave a little one aside, is to leave God aside. The little one is the person who particularly needs us to live.

Thus, in the Gospel of Mark, we see Jesus angry at the Pharisees and other Jews who, by their law, gave man permission not to come to help their parents in need: "'…Whatever support you might have had from me is Corban' (that is, an offering to God)—then you no longer permit doing anything for a father or mother, thus making void the word of God through your tradition that you have handed on. And you do many things like this" (Mk 7:11–13). To turn away from someone who is in need in favor of God is, in reality, to turn away from the Lord.

That is what the Curé of Ars tells us: "You want to pray to the Good God, to spend your day in the church; but you think that it would be useful to work for a few poor people that you know and who are in great need: that is much more pleasing to God than your day spent at the foot of the holy tabernacles."

Each day, we rub shoulders with poor people of all kinds. Often, we ask ourselves how we should act. John Vianney teaches us not to judge what has led these people to find themselves in this situation. Have we not heard the same said on the subject of the unemployed, the same criticism that the Curé of Ars noted: "You are so lazy! You could work. You are young. You have strong arms"? It is not for us to judge, but to help— short-term help to assist them in their immediate needs, long-term help through educating both mankind and society.

THE "PROVIDENCE" OF ARS

John Vianney lived a spirit of welcome to others in a very special way with the young girls of Ars and the surrounding region. First set up as a free school, "Providence" house (the *Providence*) became an orphanage for the abandoned girls from the surrounding villages. His concern for the education of the young children was a true form of love and help to the poorest, for education permits a person to be conscious of his own dignity and to not be exploited in either his life or work.

By welcoming the girls, and later, by supporting the opening and functioning of a free school for boys, the Curé of Ars acted in a long-term manner. He knew that the children would, one day, be mothers and fathers who would have to raise and educate their own children, both in the secular and religious areas. For the first place where a child is educated is in the family. The parents are the children's first teachers. It is thus through the school and the catechism that John Vianney trained the children and young people for their future responsibilities as parents.

Our consciousness of our filiation to the Father through Jesus Christ and of our mission as baptized believers experienced through the Holy Spirit stimulates us in love for others. It helps us to do everything so that no one finds himself, one day, on the wrong side of the path of life, either by a lack of affection and presence of parents or by a lack of education, food, and civil peace, and so on. It is a mission that we have to undertake together, in the Church.

To personally live a welcome to others is not a simple task, and it never will be. In order to do it, we must accept a form of self-renunciation, an attitude of "each for his own" that we have throughout our entire lives. Self-renunciation does not mean to "sacrifice yourself" for others by silencing within ourselves everything that could be judged as feelings, desires, aspirations, or personal callings. For to act in this manner is to destroy oneself and to run the enormous risk of investing everything in another person to the point of suffocating him, to not allow him to be himself, so much so that, in return, we await a "reward" for the "sacrifice" of our life we have made for that other person.

Love for another is true in as much as it is first a love of self. "You shall love your neighbor as yourself" (Mk 12:31). Let us not forget the second part of that phrase. The more we are "comfortable with ourselves" by loving ourselves just as we are and with our own limitations (which is different from our sins), the more we have the capacity, within us, to love others, all others. True sacrifice is a gift, an offering of self through love for another person. And in the first place, an offering of self to the Lord. It is love which guides an act of offering, and not a "need to sacrifice oneself because the religion demands it," as we sometimes hear.

WELCOMING ENEMIES

The Curé of Ars wanted to love everyone in the world, without exception, including the people of the village who were against him and over whom, as their parish priest, he had the pastoral responsibility. That also included his brother priests who didn't understand how he practiced his ministry. He was not spared from criticism, humiliation, jealousy, and opposition from them. He said: "It's not austerity that weakens me, slander is hurtful in other ways."

At times, do we, ourselves, experience both open and hidden acts of aggression caused by work or study colleagues, neighbors, friends, or family? In as much as these acts are truly unjustified, we are tempted to shrug our shoulders. Let us look at the Curé of Ars; his behavior becomes a veritable education for us as he draws his strength from prayer before the Lord. He said: "They don't think that they are doing something bad. I increased my politeness and thoughtfulness towards them and I gave more alms to those I was in the habit of helping." And this other advice: "He truly said something that hurt me, and I truly prayed to God for him. I must take care of him."

With John Vianney, let us contemplate Christ on the cross, the Righteous One who was unjustly condemned: "Father, forgive them; for they do not know what they are doing" (Lk 23:34). On the cross, Jesus put into practice his own words about loving our enemies. Let us together realize this well-known passage from the Gospel, which is often difficult to live in our daily lives: "You have heard that it was said, 'You shall love your neighbor and hate your enemy.' But I say to you, Love your enemies and pray for those who persecute you, so that you may be children of your Father in heaven…" (Mt 5:43–45).

Like the Curé of Ars, it is in prayer that we can draw the strength to stand fast when faced with trials. But first, let us ask the Lord and discern with someone able to counsel us if we are justly or falsely reproached. For it could happen that we don't always walk in the right direction along the path to the Gospel!

If the Lord confirms that we are truly faithful to the evangelical life, then we can integrate these trials into a path of spiritual life by leading us to an even more total self-abandonment into the hands of the Lord. This path could experience a "night of faith"; but let us believe that if it is a spiritual desert for us, we are not alone. God is there, even if it is during the night.

REFLECTION QUESTIONS

Am I ever called to leave my prayer time because someone needs my help? How do I respond to this call? Do I view it as a distraction, or as an opportunity to expand my silent prayer into active prayer? As a Christian, how welcoming and approachable am I to someone who might need help? Do I seek that person out myself or wait for that person to ask me for assistance? What is my opinion of the poor and needy? How do I perceive/judge/observe their needy state? Do I hold prejudices towards such people that I might want to address?

DAY TEN

The Place of the Laity

FOCUS POINT

There is a common misconception within the Church that ministry (that is, service to the parish, the Church) is reserved for the hierarchy or religious men and women. This is simply not true. All of us—religious *and* lay people—are called to serve God by serving one another. God has given each one of us particular gifts that he calls us to use—not just in our workaday lives, but in our service and ministry to others in the parish realm. We should never hesitate to offer our gifts for service to God and his Church when we see an opportunity to do so.

The surest way to light the fire of our Lord's love in the hearts of the faithful is to explain to them the Gospel, this book of love where our Lord shows himself, in each line, as loving and tender, patient, humble, and always the consoler and friend of

*mankind, speaking only to him about love and his commit-
ment to give himself completely to him, and only responding
to him through love.*

I t is because of the "desire for God," the sense and hunger
for prayer developed in the hearts of some of the men and
women of the village, that John Vianney began his mission
with the laity. It was on these spiritual foundations that he
then developed a pastoral plan that aimed at giving the greatest number of people some parish responsibility, as much for
the material as for the spiritual plan.

The place of the laity in the parish life of Ars was not just
a simple sharing of responsibilities between people of good
will. It was a true mission granted by the Curé to one person
or another, after certain discernment, which would, by the rico-
chet effect, eventually reach all of the parishioners of Ars.

THE SPIRITUAL PASTORAL PLAN

Our mission as baptized believers is rooted in the contemplation of the Lord. It is the basis, the foundation of all apostolic
life. We can't proclaim the death and resurrection of Jesus Christ
if we don't take the time to go back to the source, to "meet"
him, the one in whom we put our faith and hope. If we are
committed to a charitable activity of any kind, it is from the
trinitarian God that we draw the strength to act.

Christian life is not just a putting into action of an ideol-
ogy, it is the practical consequence of our love for someone:
Jesus Christ, the Son of God the Savior, died and arisen, in
whom we dwell and who dwells in us with the Father, through

the Holy Spirit. That is what Festus said to King Agrippa (in the Acts of the Apostles) when he was explaining why Paul was in prison in Caesarea: "When the accusers stood up, they did not charge him with any of the crimes that I was expecting. Instead they had certain points of disagreement with him about their own religion and about a certain Jesus, who had died, but whom Paul asserted to be alive" (Acts 25:18–19).

No matter what path permitted our loving meeting with the Lord, we are led to put our faith and hope in the trinitarian God of love who is Father, Son, and Holy Spirit.

But faith without action is "dead" faith, as Saint James' letter states: "a person is justified by works and not by faith alone" (Jas 2:24). That is why, after having based his pastoral plan on the quality of the spiritual life of his parishioners, the Curé of Ars would call some of them to perform true missions of evangelization, through the education of the children.

THE EDUCATIONAL PASTORAL PLAN

Although nothing facilitated the task, most particularly the financial side, John Vianney decided to open a free school for girls, called the *Providence*. He was always concerned with the scholastic and spiritual education of children. After thinking about it, and intuitively knowing that the best evangelization of the girls of the region would be done by local girls (that would later be the idea for Catholic Action), he called upon two young women from Ars to perform this mission of education. He sent them to be trained in Fareins, with the Sisters of Saint Joseph of Lyons. It is with these two from the village that he would educate the children of the *Providence*.

We know that this wasn't easy for the locals to accept, but education and catechism were essential. Later, he would say:

"They said many things against the *Providence*. They said that the children were badly looked after, yet God performed many miracles for them and nothing was lacking." How true that was!

The Curé of Ars did the same for the boys' school. He sent a young man to be trained for three years. There, once again, he wanted a free school and didn't hesitate to finance it for a time himself.

Prayer to be able to do the work of God, a discernment for people, the concern for training that is adapted to people, and entrusting a mission to them—that was the approach that the Curé of Ars had towards many of his parishioners. Today, in the Church, we must live this approach. For God calls each of us to fulfill a precise mission. Everyone is not an expert in everything, and if no one is indispensable, then anyone can't replace anyone else.

Through the way we practice our mission as baptized believers, we give witness to our brothers and sisters about who God is. Through our words and our actions, we teach others without even knowing it. Only the spiritual life helps us "practice" our baptismal promise and our mission in the Church, according to what God wants. Let us not take the risk of walking backwards on the path of the Christian mission by leaning on our own ideas and skills, no matter how good they may be. The Lord also has his say!

THE PASTORAL PLAN OF SERVICE

As the "spiritual pastoral plan" of the Curé of Ars and his own spiritual life brought fruit, pilgrims began to come in droves. There again, John Vianney put his parish "into action" in order to welcome the visitors. He called upon two men, giving one the responsibility to open a hotel for the pilgrims and the other to assure transportation for them between Lyons and Ars. They were missions that were very concrete, very material, but very necessary to the life of the village.

The pastoral initiatives to give the laity of the parish responsibility were more numerous than have been cited here. But these are good examples to show just to what point the Curé of Ars can help us open our eyes about what is happening today and challenge us to take the initiative in our own lives, after praying and discerning the will of the Lord.

His entire pastoral plan was oriented to one person: Jesus Christ. Using all means available, yet never forcing anyone, he tried to show the face of God to man. It was a face of God that wanted man's happiness, who was attentive to man's needs; a face that reconciled man as a sinner with love and brought him interior peace.

The Curé of Ars overlooked nothing to proclaim the Good News. He never hesitated to lend a hand, whether it was to beat the wheat with the parishioners who were farmers, raise the walls of the chapels of the church with the masons of the village, or even clean the toilets in the *Providence.*

The Son of God made himself become man to lead mankind to God the Father. Through his ministry, the holy Curé teaches us, today, to live close to people, not to get lost amongst them, but through this proximity, to touch those who are the farthest from the Church. In Jesus Christ, God was incarnated. Mankind is important to God, for through their lives, he speaks to them. That is why our life can become the word of God for man today, if we nourish our life with the love of God, through contemplation.

The place of the laity in the Church is not acquired through a battle against the hierarchy. It is established through the desire of each person to do God's work so that the ministries complement each other. Again, we must agree to utter a total "yes" to the Lord, with his will to let it speak within us, to let it inspire us as to what he wants to do through us, and believe that, through his Holy Spirit, he can also speak in the hearts of others. To live in the Church is to look together in the same direction, God's direction. It is to accept that the Holy Spirit speaks to each of our hearts and not only to those of a few. That is true for the two directions: the laity towards the hierarchy of the Church and the hierarchy towards the laity in the Church.

REFLECTION QUESTIONS

What is my understanding of the role of the laity in the Church? Might I consider reading what Vatican Council II has stated concerning the role of the laity in the Church? How involved am I in the day-to-day life of my parish community? What steps might I take to become more involved in my parish, so that the gifts God has given me will be put to the best possible use? Might I consider speaking with my parish priest or parish volunteer coordinator about opportunities available in the parish that will address my desire to share my gifts with others for the greater glory of God?

DAY ELEVEN

To Live in the Church

FOCUS POINT

The Church is our guide, it is our teacher, it is our family. Our support comes from the Church, for when we stumble in sin, the Church—instituted by Jesus Christ, guided by the Holy Spirit—is there to encourage our reconciliation with God, whom we have offended, and the people we have harmed. We are always called to return to the flock, under the care of our great Shepherd. The Church is firm in its teaching; it aids its members in purifying their hearts, accepting what is of God and rejecting anything less than God. Like Mary, the Church says "yes" to God and gives itself totally to him.

In the unity of the love of God, the hearts of Christians are reunited, and this unity is heaven. How beautiful!

O beautiful union of the Church on earth with the Church in heaven!

The perfect Christian is that person who unites all of their actions, worries, prayers, and beats of their heart with the merits of the entire Church.... That is just like the person who gathers straw into a pile and lights it: the flame goes very high, it becomes a furnace. But if we only set one piece of straw on fire, it puts itself out right away.

The Curé of Ars spoke little of the Church. On the other hand, he lived a very close union with it, insofar as it is as much Church-communion as it is Church-institution. The connection with the Church begins with the same faith that is shared and experienced; faith in God the Father, the Son, and the Holy Spirit; faith in the trinitarian God of love, proclaimed during both good and bad times for the Church from the beginning of the first Christian community to today; faith in God and communion among Christians.

The divisions that occurred between Christians throughout the centuries were not God's will, but the fruit of Christian attitudes that strayed. They are like an open wound in the body of Christ and in his Body which is the Church. To heal these wounds is a mission for today and the future for, as long as they remain, they will offer a conflicting message to the world. But as we have seen in the previous days, it is not by a test of strength between us that unity will happen, but through opening hearts only to the will of the Lord.

"THAT THEY MAY BE ONE"

We all know this prayer that Jesus prayed before his arrest: "Holy Father, protect them in your name that you have given me, so that they may be one, as we are one…. I ask not only on behalf of these, but also on behalf of those who will believe in me through their word, that they may all be one. As you, Father, are in me and I am in you, may they also be in us, so that the world may believe that you sent me" (Jn 17:11, 20–21).

The unity of the Church—that is, the disciples of Christ—doesn't consist of living in a rigid uniformity. Rather, it is similar to a multitude of flowers, each being unique, yet together, they form a harmony. In order to live, each flower draws from the same source of living water: Christ. It is he who makes our unity. Harmony is possible thanks to the acceptance of the difference and singularity of each one. Each baptized believer brings a new richness to the bouquet that is the Church, through their personality and practice of the Gospel.

In the same way that the Father is not the Son yet they are "one" in love, in the Church, the unity of Christians is not due to their uniformity, but to their union in God who is Love. Difference is not a source of division, but an expression of the variety of the gifts from the Holy Spirit…if this is lived in love! That is what the Curé of Ars expresses in the first phrase cited at the beginning of this day of prayer.

Inasmuch as we know that we are loved by God and we agree to be loved, we can grow in unity, in spite of our diversities. "If we only knew how much the Lord loves us, we would die from pleasure! I don't believe that there are hearts hard enough to not love when they see themselves loved so much!" said John Vianney. The Church exists through love and can only give witness by living in the love of God and mankind. Otherwise, it will become, and thus we will become, a simple human organization where each person sees things from their own point of view and not that of God's.

THE CHURCH'S TEACHING

The Church in its institution—in particular the bishops, successors to the apostles—has the mission to guide God's people in their faith and love of the Trinity. As a function of this love that God has for man and the covenant sealed in Jesus Christ, the Church brings to each of us its reflection about different areas of life. This could help us to be more aware of what is happening around us and make us attentive to the fact that societal values aren't always evangelical values.

John Vianney spoke words, with respect to certain human behaviors, that were incensed: "They give up their eternity for the fluff of the world." He had no back door when it came to telling us what he thought—that was essentially due to his sharply honed consciousness of God's love for mankind. For him, it was an interior rupture to see just to what point man destroys himself through following the quick pleasures of the world when God offers him a love that is pure. But we do know that it is easier to let ourselves be carried away by the desires of the moment than to renounce them through faithfulness to the love of the Lord.

Each of us needs the support of the Church to be faithful to the life of the Lord. And if the Church keeps watch over certain aspects of man's life in our era, it isn't to stop us from living by putting "forbidden" signs everywhere; rather, it's to guide us by putting a parapet on each side of the bridge of life. The holy Curé said: "Happy is the Christian who is educated and enters into the spirit of the Church."

The Church is at the service of all mankind, but to be at

the service does not mean that it must say "yes" to all man's desires and fantasies. It is the image of Christ the servant, who gave his life for the multitude. Christ's service was his words and his life that led man to the Father. It was a service that awakened the conscience to the notions of good and evil, with reference to God and not as a function of our human laws. That is what we read in Psalm 51 of the liturgy of the Church: "Against you, you alone, have I sinned, and done what is evil in your sight" (Ps 51:4). It is only with reference to the Lord and his Word that we can say what is evil and good in our lives. Through its reflections and teachings, the Church helps us to enter into this knowledge of the love of God that will purify our hearts of the false lights or false desires that could dwell there, and give it to the One, the living source of all love.

OBEDIENCE

The Curé of Ars always considered his connection to the bishop as an indication of his total attachment to Christ. We find this connection shown at the ordination of a deacon and priest through the question asked by the bishop: "Do you promise to live in communion with me and my successors in respect and obedience?" This promise does not mean an abandonment of thought and personal reflections in order to become a "shadow" of the thinking of the bishop. It is to recognize the authority of the bishop since he is a successor of the apostles, in order to proclaim the Good News in communion with the entire Church and to guide the local church as a father through his love for God and his proclamation of the Gospel.

Throughout his life and ministry as the Curé of Ars, John Vianney showed us that obedience to the bishop is not passive submission but a relationship that is experienced through dialogue, in the knowledge that as a last recourse, the decision rests with the bishop. The example of the *Providence* schooling house illustrates this well. The bishop of Belley asked the Curé of Ars to relinquish the *Providence* to the Sisters of Saint Joseph of Bourg in order to ensure the future of the house. Refusing at first, it was only after long discussions and the assurance of certain guarantees that John Vianney accepted, bowing before the insistence of the bishop. He said: "I don't see the will of God in it, but Monsignor does. We have no other choice but to obey."

If the bishop occupies the place of Christ in the government of the Church, he is not, however, Christ. The mission received and signified in the sacrament of ordination doesn't guarantee the infallibility of the thoughts and actions of man. Consequently, this is also true for each of us, in our mission as baptized believers or even for one of us, in the fulfillment of a specific mission received in the Church. If we don't have the desire to do God's work, nor let him work in us as he wishes, even if we participate in all the sacraments of the Church, it would be difficult for them to produce any fruit in us.

The history of the Church shows us that its children, at times, had difficulty remaining faithful to the Gospel. That is due to the weaknesses and, above all, the sins that, at times, dwell in the hearts of the baptized believers. Knowing that we are, at the same time, sinners forgiven by the Lord and messengers of an extraordinary mission received from God himself, we could only begin by praying for each other, and more specifically, for those who have special responsibilities in the Church. That is what we experience, for example, during Mass when we pray for the pope, our bishop and all the bishops, the priests, deacons, and all baptized believers.

Let us pray and ask the Lord to give us the desire to do his work, his will. It is our responsibility to say a complete "yes" to God, and to remain faithful to our commitment. It is also our responsibility to alert the Church, through its bishops, priests, religious, or concerned laity, when we have a certain interior conviction, which has been discerned and verified through prayer, that they are mistaken or have taken a wrong turn in the practice of the Good News. At times, some say: "It is better to be mistaken in the Church than to be right outside of the Church." And if we mean, by the word *Church*, the men and women who make it up, that is an error. For if the Holy Spirit shows us that the Church is mistaken in its pastoral practices, it is our duty through our love for the Church to make it aware of this. For to act in this manner is not to deny the Church, but just the opposite, to want it to be holy in its membership and irreproachable before God. "Christ loved the church and gave himself up for her, in order to make her holy by cleansing her with the washing of water by the word, so as to present the church to himself in splendor, without a spot or wrinkle or anything of the kind—yes, so that she may be holy and without blemish" (Eph 5:25–27).

REFLECTION QUESTIONS

How do I view the Church in my own life? Do I view the Church as a taskmaster, telling me what to do, when to do it, and reprimanding me when I fail to do so? Or do I view the Church as a guide, leading me through the difficulties of life, helping me to choose wisely what is good and of God; helping me to see what temptations are less than God so that I might reject what is not helpful to my spiritual life? Do I make efforts to seek the Church's guidance on matters that face me? Might I make it a practice to read from the *Catechism of the Catholic Church* or the documents of Vatican Council II?

DAY TWELVE

Proclaim the Gospel

FOCUS POINT

We are called to evangelize by the very fact that we are Christians. We are called to invite others into the hope, love, and understanding we share with the Church. Evangelization is often thought of as a public proclamation having to do with large crowds. While this is true in some cases, most of us are called to a type of evangelization that is much quieter, but with, we hope, just as much impact. It is by the little things we do and say, and the happiness with which we live our lives, that people will be drawn to the Good News of God and his Church—they will want the happiness and communion they see in us.

The Word of God is not a little thing! The last words of our Lord to his apostles, "Go into all the world and proclaim the

good news to the whole creation" (Mk 16:15), were to make
us see that the Word passes before everything. What makes us
know the Church? The words that we have heard. What makes
us know what is important? The Word. What makes mothers
and fathers know what duties they have to do for their chil-
dren, and children know what they must do for their parents?
The Word. Why are we so blind and ignorant? Because we
give no value to the Word of God.

▬▬▬

J ohn Vianney didn't see the world and God as conflicting.
The world of mankind is called to live the bounty of its ex-
istence in union with the Lord. But this bounty of life is only
possible through the knowledge of and welcome given to divine love. To know that we are loved by God, that is the path
of life! For us, love is not reserved for just a few. For Christ
gave his life for all—the humankind of yesterday, today, and
tomorrow—so all could enter into communion through him
with the Father and live eternally in the perfection of shared
love. For the Curé of Ars, it wasn't a world from which to
escape because it was mired in sin, but the world in which we
live and that we must open to the love of God and each of us.

"WHOM SHALL I SEND?"

John Vianney burned with love for this God of tenderness and
mercy, fully revealed in Christ and proclaimed by the Church.
He was like the prophet Isaiah who, after having been touched
by God, "heard the voice of the Lord saying, 'Whom shall I
send, and who shall go for us?' [and he replied] 'Here I am;
send me!'" (Isa 6:8).

The Curé of Ars was not content to just "bring around" his parish. He wanted to proclaim the Gospel in its totality; that is, all the way to leading hearts to the union with God on this earth; a union through love. He said: "to be united with God! Let us seek to be united and to unite. Human speech is filled with unity. Error is the obstacle to union, there is no union possible between wrong and truth." It is a union that draws its source in the unity of the Holy Trinity, which crosses the heart of man and materializes in charity. First, the Curé of Ars put his words into practice: "Our Curé did all that he said, he practiced all that he taught," said the witnesses.

The proclamation of the Gospel is everyone's mission as baptized believers. We are not asked to convert, but to give witness through our words and actions. It is God who converts hearts. But conversion is only possible if there is proclamation, and the proclamation happens through the word. Without actions, our words are cut off, but without words, our actions alone cannot express their reasons for acting. The word is the necessary passage for the proclamation of the Good News. Thus, our words carry life when they are converted and united to God. But they are also sowers of the seeds of division and death when they are not controlled. "But now you must get rid of all such things—anger, wrath, malice, slander, and abusive language from your mouth. Do not lie to one another, seeing that you have stripped off the old self with its practices and have clothed yourselves with the new self, which is being renewed in knowledge according to the image of its creator" (Col 3:8–10).

It is the union with God that is the starting point for any change in both the interior and exterior life, and all conversions in our human interpersonal and collective relationships. As Christians, we do not have to wait until the other person is converted before we have a newly established relationship with him in Christ. From today on we must live our faith in the midst of the world, knowing the risk we are taking to be received as lambs amongst the wolves...wolves that, at times, call themselves Christians!

TO SAY GOD WITH ALL OUR BEING

That is what the Curé of Ars lived: to say God by means of his entire person. Such was his relationship with God, as was it with others, that he wanted this same relationship for others. For even if the proclamation of the Gospel passes, as we have come to see, in words, it will also be transmitted by the entire being. Our actions aren't only for a certain person or group. We can "say God" by our way of looking at another person, listening to them, speaking to them, and loving them.

John Vianney said the following to the members of his parish confraternities: "Don't make a mistake; you, as confreres and religious brothers, are obligated to lead a life that is more perfect than regular Christians." Going back to what he said, we could say that, as baptized believers, we are obligated to lead a more perfect life than regular mortals. "Like obedient children, do not be conformed to the desires that you formerly had in ignorance. Instead, as he who called you is holy, be holy yourselves in all your conduct; for it is written, 'You shall be holy, for I am holy'" (1 Pet 1:14–16).

In commitments and decisions we make, we can equally proclaim God. That is why we must let all decisions that concern our future ripen in prayer. Then the moment for "a leap of faith" comes, that is, a time when nothing can absolutely tell us that a certain decision is a good one. The Lord can inspire us in our heart or show us, through an intermediary, what is good. But then the act of trust is necessary, especially when we are later criticized.

That is similar to what the Curé of Ars experienced with the *Providence*. Every day, he had to find the money to feed its residents, local girls as well as the orphans that came from everywhere. Who could say, "on the spot," with a "market study" in their hands, that the Curé was right to get into such a venture? No one. Only through faith was the holy Curé able to hold his ground in spite of material difficulties, "improvised" management, and, at times, criticism from certain people. It's only with hindsight that we can confirm that the work of God was truly done here. It is the same for certain decisions we may make in faith. Nothing guarantees that it is truly a work of God. Only the future may eventually provide proof in our favor. But, at times, we have to take the chance, for if we wait until the "time" is favorable, if we wait to have all possible guarantees of success, we will do nothing at all.

The proclamation of the Gospel is a risk, the risk of not being received favorably. God took this risk: "He was in the world, and the world came into being through him; yet the world did not know him. He came to what was his own, and his own people did not accept him. But to all who received him, who believed in his name, he gave power to become children of God" (Jn 1:10–12).

THE "MISSIONS" TO EVANGELIZE

The Curé of Ars began his pastoral plan by rooting it in the spiritual life; both his and that of many of his parishioners. Just as a stone that is thrown in the water causes a series of waves to radiate further and further away, thus the desire to unite man to God caused the Curé of Ars to have a vitality and missionary radiance that went beyond the borders. The first effects of his pastoral plan obviously touched Ars, but very quickly, through the help of the priests in neighboring parishes, and his participation in "missions," the people of the neighboring towns and villages were touched by a renewal of their love of God.

The missions were times of intense prayer, proclamation of the Gospel, confessions, and visitations, sponsored for a few days for a parish by the diocesan priests and missionaries. This all costs money, for these people must eat, and so on. The Curé of Ars, seeing the numerous benefits of this pastoral activity, financed a hundred or so of these missions in the diocese of Belley and even outside of it. He said: "We always find enough people to buy banners or statues, but the preference should be for the salvation of souls through missions. You don't know all of the good that they do. In order to appreciate their effect, you must be in my shoes, as a confessor."

If the missions, such as the Curé experienced, no longer happen today, we do, however, see the same effects in other formats—the increase in the number of personal spiritual retreats, for example, the collection to which this book belongs to is yet another. We need to draw our support from the Lord again and again, go to him as we go to a spring, and draw some of the living water of his love that flows in abundance for all mankind. God made himself our "food" and "drink," our "communion" so that humanity might live the mission he received from God in truth: to love.

We are given the responsibility to proclaim the One who is "the way, and the truth, and the life" (Jn 14:6), Jesus, who leads us to the bounty of a relationship with the eternal Father through the gift of the Holy Spirit of communion. Through this, have no fear of being filled with and changed by his love. Without him, we can do nothing. With him, hope is possible!

REFLECTION QUESTIONS

How do I evangelize in my own life? How do I proclaim the Good News to people in need, people who are struggling in their relationship with God? Might a kind word, a helpful act, a compassionate gesture introduce that person to the love I feel for God (and want them to feel as well)? What role does Scripture play in my spiritual life? Might reading the Bible on a daily basis (if even for just five minutes) benefit my spiritual life as I seek to evangelize by the Christian example I am living?

The Christian Family

FOCUS POINT

The family is our first model of God's love. We come to know the qualities of God through our time with our families. These qualities of love, generosity, and kindness are not, of course, as immense as God's love, generosity, and kindness, but we are given a taste of this (hopefully) during our childhood, within a family setting. There are those, though, who are not so fortunate as to taste God's love in a loving family environment. It is our hope as the Church that these people will be shown God's love by their extended family, us, the Body of Christ.

The sacrament of marriage, which is so great and holy in the eyes of God, only produces its effects in those who receive it with the proper intentions. We mustn't marry like pagans who don't know God. What does one see in the world today? Alas!

We take a woman out of convenience, through ambition, or because of her beauty. We have the wedding, give ourselves to happiness...and then everything is said! And we want to be happy. Oh no, it's not possible. The Good God does not bless unions in which he has not been consulted. Even in happy marriages, let there be no illusions, there are worries and often great ones. Each person has their own imperfections and faults.

W e are not in the habit of meditating with the Curé of Ars on the subject of couples, parents, children, and the family. Yet, his holiness shines all the way into our homes, where his words can educate and support us today, almost a century and a half after his death. In a language that is always simple and full of images, he brings out the fundamental realities of love and the education of children. He, the lover of God, undoubtedly has something to say to us about what is the foundation of true human love and the way to be loved in the Christian family.

TO LOVE IS TO GIVE OF ONESELF

We see that for the Curé of Ars, there is no true love if the man "marries her out of convenience, through ambition, or because of her beauty," for the woman is not an object in the service of man and his desires. That seems evident, yet popular songs don't seem to give us that impression. It seems that humans have become objects of desire and possession today; one look becomes a leer and a multitude of messages are exchanged, none of which give the correct perception of what God truly created. The other person doesn't count; what is important seems to be my own personal pleasure. Is this love? Or is it something we experience with another when we want it?

"God created humankind in his image, in the image of God he created them; male and female he created them" (Gen 1:27). In all that God created, only the human being was created in his image. Not a physical image, which is secondary, but an image at heart. In the very depth of man, in his most inner place, his being is the "image" of God. That is, by seeing man live and act according to the will of God, we can discover that God is love.

We love another inasmuch as we love them as God loves us: through proposing it to another and awaiting their "yes" with immense respect. We can't impose our love on someone else, we can only respect them. The thing that will allow our love to grow and be kept under control is taking time to speak to one another. It is a sharing with one another, where each person discovers the other through confident discussion, where each welcomes the other as he or she is, without seeking to change them. To love someone is not to love the image we have of them, or the one we want to have, it's to love them in reality, just as they are. The Curé of Ars reminds us that "each person has their own imperfections and faults."

Our love reaches its fullest in the gift of self to the other. For if we are sincere, our love becomes a commitment; if not, it isn't love, just the pleasure of being together. The commitment is the gift of self to the other through love, a reciprocal gift. It is a gift of great value, a unique gift that we give to someone we love. We are this gift. And when this gift is given, we can't take it back. When the gift of our body is given, it can't be taken back. Our heart is the greatest gift that we could ever offer, and our body is a very concrete and visible expression of it. Through our body, we don't give something, we give ourselves totally. And faithfulness is the indication of this total gift.

This is how we live our resemblance to God, who gives nothing, but who gives himself in fullness to mankind, even through his body on the cross, and in the Eucharist. God gives himself and doesn't take it back. In this way our love, taught through the love of God, doesn't take itself back after having been given. That is why it is so important for us not to just throw ourselves into anyone's arms, nor to leap blindly into marriage. Love is a commitment that is such a great commitment for a person that they have to prepare for it and let it ripen before they give themselves to it completely.

PARENTS, THE FIRST TEACHERS

The education of children has always posed certain problems for parents because each child has his or her own personality, and are not the executors of their parents' wishes. Simply said, they are themselves. If to educate someone is to teach them to become responsible for themselves and others, then education is a fundamental mission. And the first teachers of life are the parents. We all know that there is no magic recipe for success in education; on the other hand, there are a few fundamental rules that we must remember.

John Vianney was also once a child. As a priest, he often visited families in Ars, and he knew them well. He saw what was happening regarding the education of the children. That is what permitted him to often say what he thought, to help parents in their duty as teachers. Thus, what he said bears repeating: "Your children remember much more about what they see you do than what you've told them to do." We could call it a universal truth, but something that connects with what we have already meditated on in the preceding days: our words of faith in God truly become a witness inasmuch as we live what we say and what we believe. If we ask our children to love their brothers and sisters and we are, at our own level, divisive with our own siblings because of an inheritance, for example, what weight do our words have? That is what the Curé of Ars said: "It would be very self-indulgent to forbid your children to do what you do yourself!"

Parents have an irreplaceable and fundamental role in the education of the family. Their example is the best teacher. John Vianney said: "Virtue passes from the mother's heart into the heart of the children who willingly do what they see is being done." When he speaks about prayer, he compares it to "a gentle conversation between a child and his father." These are words that show us and remind us just how important dialogue is between the father and mother and their children. Yes, education passes through that meeting.

Thus, a child is thought to have a good life if he has many material goods, plays in many different sports, or participates in cultural or artistic activities; but if he doesn't see his parents very often, he doesn't have the chance to experience the relationship, participate in long sessions of discussion and just spend time with them, and he will suffer in his heart. He will not have the experience of family happiness and runs the serious risk of filling the void in his life with an escape into substance abuse...maybe all the way to a cry for help through an attempted suicide. The Curé has a terrible thought on this subject: "You take better care of your animals in the stables...than you do of your poor children!" It is a terrible reality that expressed his suffering at seeing how many children are in such great need of love and who grow up second in importance after their parents' jobs. Is this not a call from the Lord addressed to the world today? Do you see yourself here?

THE PRAYERS OF CHILDREN

The Curé of Ars always believed in the strength of the prayers of children. Often, he confided his prayer intentions to the little girls in his school. The witnesses said: "He made the little children of the *Providence* pray for the graces he wanted to obtain and said that they were always granted." He said: "They are small, but their prayers are big to God. To not let the children pray is to steal a great pleasure away from the Good God."

If we believe that mankind was created in God's image, who carries, right from the time of conception, the life of God in him, this means that, very early on, children can have a spiritual relationship with the Lord. For if we must wait to see if the child can intellectually understand what God is in order to speak to him about the Lord, we will never speak to him about God. But the relationship he has with God is not an intellectual one, but one of feeling, a relationship in the heart. Our love for someone grows inasmuch as we meet with them and they like it. It is the same with God: it is by meeting with him through prayer, for example as a family, that the child will discover, little by little, who God is, and learn to tell him of his love, with respect to the age of the child. Also with respect to his age is his natural trust in someone else, who is great. "Let the little children come to me; do not stop them; for it is to such as these that the kingdom of God belongs. Truly I tell you, whoever does not receive the kingdom of God as a little child will never enter it" (Mk 10:14–15).

REFLECTION QUESTIONS

How has my experience of family helped to shape my understanding of God's love for his creation? What other qualities of God have I tasted growing up in my family? How do I express these qualities in my own life? How do I share God's love with others? How do I express the mercy and forgiveness I have received from God when dealing with someone who has wronged me? Am I generous to others as I have known God's generosity? Do I set a good Christian example by my words, and particularly my actions, for the children I encounter in my daily life?

DAY FOURTEEN

Priests

FOCUS POINT

God calls priests from among the members of the Body of Christ. John Vianney heard this call and persevered through his studies, finally arriving at ordination to the priesthood as God had willed. As a priest, the Curé of Ars ministered with great devotion to the people of his diocese. Like all good priests and all holy people, John Vianney recognized the importance of meeting each person he encountered right where they were spiritually, loving them for who they were right there, and paying attention to and addressing their individual needs.

You could have two hundred angels there and they cannot pardon you. But a priest, as simple as he may be, can do it. He can say to you: "Go in peace, I forgive you." Oh, how the priesthood is something wonderful! A priest will only be understood in heaven…. If we understood him on earth, we would die, not of fright, but out of love. The priest is not a priest for himself. It isn't he who grants absolution. He, himself, doesn't administer the sacraments. He doesn't do this for himself, he does it for you. The priesthood is the love of the heart of Jesus. When you see a priest, think of our Lord.

T he ministry of the priest was something special for the Curé of Ars—not the man, the individual, but the mission that has been entrusted to him. It is the mission to reveal God, to give God, to lead people to God, to make others be born in God…. By seeing the life of the holy Curé, we understand how this ministry can take over a person completely. It requires, in order to be able to be lived, an interior availability and an authentic spiritual life on the part of the priest.

A MISSION OF THE CHURCH

John Vianney said: "The priest is not a priest for himself." In other words, a man does not decide to be a priest in order to be closer to God or for his own "personal salvation." Priests are there for all baptized believers, and also for those who have not been baptized, as well.

Everything begins, one day, when a young boy (or a man, for that matter) is awakened to the possibility to become a priest, whether it was because a priest or someone from the parish community spoke to him about it, or whether it came about after he did some reading in the Gospels, or still yet, he had seen a movie that impressed him…. It is like a gap that opens his heart to another dimension of life. He then says to himself: "Why not?"

The Church has the responsibility to discern whether this calling is truly a vocation. If it is the case, it then becomes a question of love to live. A man called to be a priest could only say "yes" to it out of love. Then, it is through their loving, their interior closeness to the Lord, that priests draw the strength to live their ministry. God is the foundation of their lives, he is their strength and support. Just as it is not enough to look at a plate of food to have it nourish us, in the same way, it is not enough only to know that God is with him in order to live the ministry of the priesthood. It is vital for him to nourish himself with the Lord, in particular, through the personal meeting experienced in prayer and the Eucharist.

The more that priests are "tuned into" God, in the same way as a television antenna is tuned into a station, the better they transmit the "new wine" of the Lord that he wants to be brought to mankind, and in the first place, to his disciples in the Church. This new wine is his Word, his Eucharist, his Pardon, and his Peace. In other words, it is he, himself. God doesn't give something for himself, he gives himself to us. In order to bring this new wine to humanity, we must not mix our own water with it, that is, moderate what comes from God with respect to our preferences or our own personal tastes. In order to "say God," there is one path: union to God, holiness.

SIGNS OF COMMUNION

The mission of priests is to "gather into one the dispersed children of God" (Jn 11:52). Each baptized person is unique, and therefore only he alone can express the fullness of life that is in God and the Church. It is the same for each human group who, themselves, can express only one aspect of this evangelical life. Yet, the person who signifies this communion between individuals and groups is the bishop, and in union with him, the priests. Signs of the presence of Christ amidst his people, the bishop and priests express, through their connection to a diversity of people and groups, that we are all members of one Body that goes beyond us: the Church.

John Vianney also shows us that the ministry of unity is lived from day to day, through meeting with people, through paying attention to each person, visiting the sick, and families…. Our ecclesiastical context, at the beginning of the twenty-first century, is different from his, but this all remains true: what is important is to meet with each person and pay attention to their individual needs. Priests must be careful to see that their ministry is not reduced to the role of a manager of Christian organizations which would cut them off from the mission they have to fulfill. And we know that the numbers of those who do not know Christ, or no longer know Christ, are numerous. With those who already live their faith daily, the priests must proclaim the Good News of the love offered.

True happiness is to be loved, know that you are loved, and accept being loved. God the Father revealed himself through Jesus Christ the Savior and guides us through the Holy Spirit. In the Holy Trinity, we find true and profound inner happiness, and not through a search for personal blossoming through the sole means of the choice of an ecologically sound life, health food, or drawing from cosmic energy, and so on.

IN SERVICE TO LOVE

"God is love" (1 Jn 4:8), and the human being finds his unity in a relationship with God. For man is not only a physical and psychological being, he is also spiritual. And he blossoms through meeting God and by the practice of fraternal love. However, we are plunged into a world that is becoming more and more pagan, seeking to unify man with the cosmos. As Christians, we know that it is not by ourselves that we enter into harmony with the universe, but through communion with God.

It is God who unifies our lives and wants our happiness through showing us the path. It is a happiness that is so strong it will last forever, a happiness over which death has no hold. The path of Life is our welcome of God's love and the practice of it. For we are profoundly loved by the Lord, and the mission of the priests, in particular, is to proclaim, explain, and, of course, live this love of God the Father, Son, and Holy Spirit.

God is not a cosmic force, he is a personal being that addresses himself to us through Jesus Christ: by the Bible, and also by the Church, inasmuch as it is "connected" to God. It is God who changes us and teaches us to live in peace and confidence with him and among ourselves, through the connection of faithful love. It is the Church, and in particular, the priests, who have this responsibility to guide each of us to the truth. This truth is not a theoretical love of God for man, but his love made visible in Jesus, God made man, born of the Virgin Mary, who suffered as a martyr on the cross, who died and rose from the dead on the third day. God loved us enough to die for us. He preferred to shed his blood in faithfulness for his love for man rather than renounce loving him. It is through the blood of Christ that we have eternal life: this blood is his life given to us through love. Jesus rose from the dead and redeemed man who refused such a great love.

Have no fear of proclaiming Jesus—God became man to lead man to God; have no fear of proclaiming the Father of all love and to whom we go and who has already met us in prayer and through our brothers and sisters; have no fear of proclaiming the Holy Spirit, the one who unites us to the Father and the Son, not through magic, but through a connection of love that has been welcomed and experienced. Have no fear of proclaiming that the sacraments of the Church are a privileged meeting with the trinitarian God of love, a meeting where God gives us his life in abundance. Have no fear, finally, to proclaim that God, who is all love, is the only one able to heal the wounds in our heart, caused particularly by the lack of love, ruptures, and the betrayals of our love we have experienced.

The mission of the priests is just that—especially in our world of today where some seek meaning for life. It is a mission with Christians who need to be enlightened by and fortified in their faith, a mission that is equally as important for all who seek God, young people and adults, and with those who have already been drawn away by the false light of some contemporary religious sect, even if they use the Bible and the teachings of Jesus. These do not lead man to a true covenant that is free and responsible with the three Persons of the Trinity.

You killed the Author of life, whom God raised from the dead. To this we are witnesses. And by faith in his name, his name itself has made this man strong whom you see and know; and the faith that is through Jesus has given him this perfect health in the presence of all of you (Acts 3:15–16).

REFLECTION QUESTIONS

Just as John Vianney was called to the priesthood, has the Lord called me to a unique vocation in my own life? What were/are some of the obstacles in following this call? Have I (like the Curé of Ars) persevered in following this call? If I am finding that following this call is a struggle, might I pray for the intercession of Saint John Vianney (who faced great struggles of his own) so that I will be graced by God with the strength to be true to my calling? I can draw great hope from the perseverance and devotion with which the Curé of Ars lived his relationship with our Lord.

DAY FIFTEEN

Death and Holiness

FOCUS POINT

When we consider how short our lives are, that death can come without warning, we must devote every moment we have to the Lord our God. Our afterlife depends upon our moral conduct and the love we live in our earthly lives. We must seek the Lord at every turn, consult him in prayer in every decision we make. We must not be filled with worry, though. We have support from all sides. Our brothers and sisters in the Church are here to support us in our challenges; we have access to the sacraments of the Church to strengthen and encourage our faith; and we have the immense love, mercy, and grace of our God all throughout our lives.

What direction will our soul take? The one we would have given it on earth. Good Christians don't die, they move a step closer to paradise. The fog that clouds our reason will be dissipated. Our spirit will have the knowledge of things that were hidden from it on earth....

We will see him! We will see him! Oh my brothers! Haven't you ever thought about it? We will see God! We will see him! We will see him just as he is...face to face! We will see him, we will see him!!!

W e live in a society where death seems to have been pushed aside. It is a taboo subject, because to speak about it is to admit our powerlessness against it. It is treated like an error that we have to hide. What is important is to remain young, get rich, be successful, and win accolades. Yet, there doesn't pass a single day when we don't hear about accidents, death, and war.... But to speak about death as one of the great events of our life is another story altogether!

WE ARE MORTAL

The only thing that is absolutely certain after birth for a human is death. The Curé of Ars said: "By dying, we make restitution. We give back to the earth what it has given us.... A small pinch of dust, the size of a nut—that is what we will become. That is truly something of which to be proud!" We are not God, we are affected by time, and thus by the limitations of time. But even if this upsets us, we must accept the fact that we will die one day. And even that could come at any minute!

However, Christian hope brings us a formidable breath of
life when faced with the trial of death. "Why do you make a
commotion and weep? The child is not dead but sleeping" (Mk
5:39), said Jesus to those who were crying at the death of the
daughter of Jairus. This is a visible sign from God to tell us
that physical death is not an end. For God, true death is the
total refusal of love. The first Christians said that those who
died in faith were "sleeping." Thus, the fear of death must not
dwell in us since we believe in the resurrection of the dead, as
happened with Jesus. It is in this sense that Jesus spoke to
Martha, crying over her brother Lazarus: "I am the resurrection and the life. Those who believe in me, even though they
die, will live, and everyone who lives and believes in me will
never die. Do you believe this?" (Jn 11:25–26).

Our fear of death is such that we do everything we can to
hide it. Certain people go to the extreme of not visiting their
parents, truly abandoning them, leaving them in a seniors'
home, a place that becomes a real "waiting room" for death,
where no one visits, because they don't want to be reminded
of their own mortality.

Physical handicaps and illness, often present at the approach
of our "eternal youth" of death, may scare us. Having neither
of these myself, I can't say how one must live them. All I can
do is express a wish: let us learn, right from today, to live within
our limitations and weaknesses, by taking our support from
God who gives us the strength to accept these things without
submitting to them. But to do that, we must renounce our
endless desire to always send a positive though false image of
ourselves to others. Often, we have something that is trou-
bling us and we make up a character. But when this facade
shatters and reality sets in, we no longer have any support. We
would prefer to be finished with life rather than live through a

failure. Let us be careful of that. Let us learn to accept ourselves and love ourselves just as we are, for God loves us with all our limitations. He doesn't wait for us to be perfect to love us. Let us learn to live our life and not submit to it or hide it from ourselves.

TO LIVE DEATH

John Vianney explained: "Death is the union with God. In heaven, the love of God will fill and flood everything." Yes, we believe it, death is not the end, but a passage, an Easter. It is an opening to the meeting with God. We will be before him just as we are, without any fireworks or parades—we, alone, face to face with God, who is all love. By then discovering with what love we are loved—an infinite love that is more personal, intense, and profound than we could ever imagine on earth— we will then understand the poverty of our male and female loves. But if, becoming aware of our sins, that is, our occasions when we lacked love, we agree to be purified by the merciful love of the Lord, then we will enter into happiness!

It is this hope of the "meeting" that gave life to the Curé. Yet he had one apprehension: to fall into despair at the moment of death. His fear of death was not due to the event of physical death, but for what death signified to him: an accounting to God of his ministry as a priest and, above all, as a parish priest. In reality, he died in God in great peace, having full consciousness that he had experienced his "poor end."

Often, we come to hear, on the subject of the way to die, "I would rather die in my sleep, so I don't notice it"; or "I would like it to happen all at once, so that I have no time to think about it." Yet, this moment is the moment of passage. We don't know under what circumstances we will die, but if we truly believe that we are going to meet the Lord, then we must ask for the grace to live our death and, as the moment approaches, to prepare ourselves for it, prepare our hearts and spirits for the eternal meeting.

PEOPLE CALLED TO HOLINESS

> And there was a great multitude that no one could count, from every nation, from all tribes and people and languages, standing before the throne and before the Lamb, robed in white, with palm branches in their hands. They cried out in a loud voice, saying, "Salvation belongs to our God, who is seated on the throne, and to the Lamb!" (Rev 7:9–10).

The hope for eternal life is not a flight from this world that is difficult to live in to plunge ourselves into a dream. Eternity is the fulfillment of the covenant with the Lord. But it is from today onwards that we must live the covenant. We are called to live the Gospel at every instant, fully rooted and invested in our daily lives. When the Church shows us saints, we discover that their holiness manifested itself on earth, concretely in their lives. The Curé of Ars said: "The saints' preaching is their example."

We are all called to holiness, all of us, without exception, for holiness is letting ourselves be loved by God, loved in a confident relationship and our practice of this love through actively showing fraternal charity. We become saints in as much as we align our lives to the will of God, the Trinity of love. The Curé also said: "The saints didn't all start off well, but they all finished well."

At the end of our fifteen days of prayer together, let us

decide to become saints through a total "yes" given freely to the Lord; a "yes" to being loved and to loving. Only God can quench our thirst for love and teach us to truly love our brothers and sisters. He is our happiness. So, let us not be afraid to become saints!

I have nothing else to prove to you than our indispensable obligation for us to become saints. If we could ask the saints, they would say that their happiness is to love God and be assured of always loving him (John Vianney).

REFLECTION QUESTIONS

As I come to the conclusion of these fifteen days of prayer, what points of inspiration can I draw from the life and spirituality of Saint John Vianney, the Curé of Ars? Might I dwell on his example of living his life as a total "yes" to the will of God? Do I recognize the great mercy of God in my own life, that I am forgiven all of my past sins, and that it is what I do in the future that counts? Can't I draw tremendous hope and optimism from John Vianney when he says, "The saints didn't all start off well, but they all finished well"? Praise God in the highest!

Bibliography

Cristiani, Leon. *Saint John Vianney: The Village Priest Who Fought God's Battles*. Pauline Books, 1977.

Ghéon, Henri. *The Secret of the Curé d'Ars*. Sheed and Ward, 1934.

LaPerchia, Alex. *Satan and the Saint: Chronicles of the Life of Saint Jean-Marie Baptiste Vianney*. Sterling House, 1999.

Rutler, George William. *The Curé D'Ars Today: Saint John Vianney*. Ignatius Press, 1988.

Sheppard, Lancelot. *Portrait of a Parish Priest: Saint John Vianney, the Curé d'Ars*. The Newman Press, 1958.

Trochu, Francis. *The Curé d'Ars*. The Newman Press, 1949.

Trouncer, Margaret. *Saint Jean-Marie Vianney: Curé of Ars*. Sheed and Ward, 1959.

Vianney, John. *The Curé of Ars and the Holy Eucharist*. Neumann Press, 2000.

———. *Sermons of the Curé of Ars*. Neumann Press, 1999.